# *UPROOTED!*
# The Argentia Story

by Eileen Houlihan

# *UPROOTED!*

# The Argentia Story

by Eileen Houlihan

Creative Publishers
St. John's, Newfoundland
1992

Appreciation is expressed to *The Canada Council* for publication assistance.

The publisher acknowledges the financial contribution of the *Department of Tourism and Culture, Government of Newfoundland and Labrador*, which has helped make this publication possible.



Front Cover: Surveyors at Argentia, circa 1942 <196> Duotone

∝ Printed on acid-free paper

Published by
CREATIVE PUBLISHERS
A Division of Robinson-Blackmore Printing & Publishing Ltd.
P.O. Box 8660, St. John's, Newfoundland A1B 3T7

Printed in Canada by:
ROBINSON-BLACKMORE PRINTING & PUBLISHING LTD.
P.O. Box 8660, St. John's, Newfoundland A1B 3T7

1st printing — November 1992
2nd printing — June 1993
3rd printing — February 1998

Canadian Cataloguing in Publication Data

Houlihan, Eileen, 1909–

Uprooted!

ISBN 1-895387-19-1

1. Argentia (Nfld.) — History.
2. Forced migration — Newfoundland — Argentia.
I. Title.

FC2199.A74H68 1992 971.8 C92-098735-4
F1124.5.A74H68 1992

CREDITS

*ONCE UPON A MINE; Story of Pre-Confederation Mines on the Island of Newfoundland* by Wendy Martin (1983)

*The Atlantic Meeting* by H. V. Morton

Provincial Archives

Freshwater Parish Records

Barbara Bailey, Placentia Librarian

Kitty McGrath

Alice Kemp

Patricia Dawson

O'Reilly Heritage House, Placentia

*Dedicated to my son William*
*and my daughter Moira.*

## Table of Contents

## Acknowledgements

*My thanks to my nephew Jim Wyse and my cousin John Hunt for the typing of the manuscript, to those who provided me with material relevant to the story, and to those former Argentia residents who so willingly shared their personal memories of the evacuation. I am especially grateful to Peggy Krachun for her interest in my writing, for giving so generously of her time and talents, and for her dealings with the publisher on my behalf. Without her valuable assistance this book may never have been published.*

## *Foreword*
by Peggy Smith Krachun

As a child I never tired of hearing my mother and father tell stories about growing up in Argentia. To me, theirs had been a magical childhood in an idyllic place of endless green meadows in summer, horse-drawn sleighs in winter, and the best climbing trees in the world. I don't think they overly romanticized it; they described it the way it was, and I supplied the romance. Yes, times were hard and they were poor—but, I believe, freer than any generation since, and close to nature in a way that I'm afraid none of us will ever be again.

I grew up experiencing a different Argentia—the Base. It was a part of our lives; we lived side by side with the Americans, went to school with them, played with them. I remember Sunday afternoons, walking the three miles or so from Freshwater to the North Rec (Recreation Centre) to enjoy the free movies, the popcorn and ice cream and chili in paper cups, the roller skating rink and the swimming pool. I remember the Christmas parties, when the schoolchildren were piled into buses and brought to the Base where Santa Claus gave each one of us a present—dolls for the girls and dump trucks for the boys. I remember the winter carnivals in the huge Miami Hangar, and riding home once in a military truck when a blizzard kept the cars off the road. Those are good memories too. "Magic" can have many meanings.

In the time between my parents' childhood and my own, a big change took place. When I was two months old we left our home in Argentia; like all the other residents, we were forced out to make way for the hasty construction of the Base for World War II. I grew up knowing this, but my sense of roots and continuity and community had to mature before I could appreciate the significance of the event on the lives of the people. And it was not until I read Eileen Houlihan's manuscript that I realized what a true cataclysm it had been.

So many who lived through that time are gone now—and it was important that the human side of this story be told firsthand, by someone who was there. I found it extremely valuable to be able to read the original letters, the reports, the transcripts of meetings—this is the way it happened, and in those exact words!

The personal accounts in Chapter 10 are such a fascinating mixture of fact, nostalgia and pathos. They reflect the tangle of conflicting emotions that must have assailed the residents at the time: the excitement of new events and new people, the anticipation of a better standard of living—but overshadowing it all, the sorrow. The stories are very moving, some in spite of—or because of?—the very simplicity with which they were told. Consider a brief entry from Mrs. Clara O'Reilly's 1941 diary: "May 27: House burned." What must have been going through her mind as she wrote those words? What was it like to be forced to leave the place of your heart? The subconscious symbolism of my aunt Rose's uprooted rosebush wasn't lost on me. I think I understand even better, now.

Mrs. Houlihan and the others have always been very clear in their own minds as to who were the real villains of this tale—the Commission of Government, the people who should have been looking out for their interests. They didn't blame the Americans, and it seems they didn't seriously question the right of a foreign government to take over their land and destroy their homes. In the global village of 1992 we've become accustomed to seeing individuals trampled by huge powers, and we've developed a good deal of scepticism. But in Argentia in 1941 their acceptance was not unusual by any means; it was widely understood that World War II had to be fought and won, and that whatever the Allies did to accomplish this was necessary and right. The Argentia people complied; they did their part, at great personal sacrifice, and were justifiably proud of their contribution.

They didn't want to stop the takeover; they only wanted recognition and consideration of their plight, and the kind of help the situation warranted. But the callous treatment they received was well illustrated in the notice to Mrs. Mary Hunt that her land was being possessed—a form letter with the salutation "Sir". Every householder, man and woman, received the same letter. War or not, emergency or not, there was no need for this kind of insensitivity, the depersonalization and trivialization of those who were already losing so much.

But they weren't all passive acquiescence and deference, by any means. Mrs. Hunt's pluck and spirit were certainly in evidence as she wrapped her late husband's hand-crafted doors in blankets and sneaked them into the truck in defiance of the rules. The gleeful ballad about the ill-fated pontoon bridge shows how little the self-assured Americans were held in awe by the Newfoundlanders. And I was gratified to learn of Father Dee's attempts to buck the huge steamroller of government in his concern for the welfare of his parishioners. How much worse would it have been if no one had fought back?

In spite of it all the Argentia people survived, and prevailed. When I look back on my own secure childhood and all the things I was able to take for granted, I see just how successful my parents and the others were in adapting to those massive changes. They picked up and built again and created a comfortable life for their families. I know now that behind their wistful meanderings into the past there must have been great heartache. As Mrs. Houlihan so eloquently points out in her epilogue, even the sunsets in the new place couldn't match the ones they had left behind.

Many years after I left Argentia that winter day in my mother's arms, I'm glad there is still more I can learn about the quiet heroism of my ancestors. I'm grateful to Mrs. Houlihan for this book, an important addition to our legacy. And I'm very, very proud to be one of the descendants of the Argentia people.

# Introduction

*It has been said that the resettlement of people from their native soil should never be forgotten. 1991 marked the fiftieth anniversary of the forced evacuation of the Argentia people from their homes to make way for the establishment of a United States Naval and Army Base during World War II. This book has been written in an effort to help the descendants of the those people to gain some knowledge of the history of Argentia, how their parents and grandparents earned their livelihood, and the trauma they experienced when they had to leave. Over half a century later, it is a fitting time to relate the Argentia story.*

Chapter One

# EARLY HISTORY OF ARGENTIA

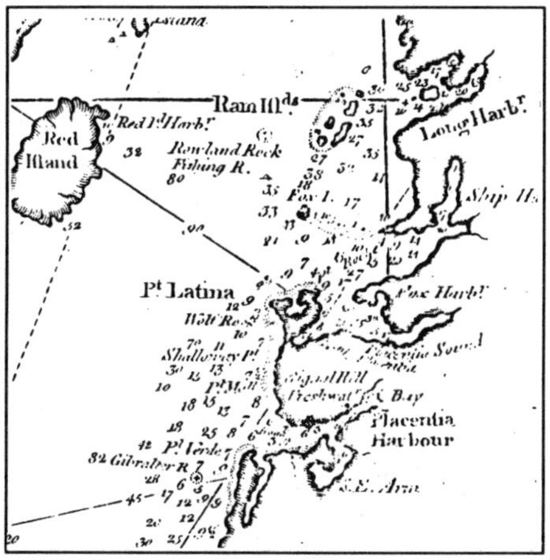

Courtesy, Centre for Newfoundland Studies, MUN

Placentia Bay, from a 1780 chart of the south-east coast of Newfoundland

For a considerable number of years after Sir Humphrey Gilbert took possession of Newfoundland for Queen Elizabeth, the island was used as a fishing station only. Settlement was forbidden, and the captain of each fishing vessel was bound under penalty to bring back every member of the crew who had sailed with him at the beginning of the season. In spite of this, many fisherman succeeded in remaining here and settling in remote places, including Placentia Bay.

It is logical to assume that some of these settled in Argentia. A Philip Power is said to have been an early settler; in all likelihood he would have been of Irish origin. Other Argentia names were: Fennessey, Traverse, Foran, Grant, Burke, O'Reilly, Hall, Cunningham, Dunphy, Evans, Murphy, Hunt, McGrath, Cleary, Smith, Kelly, Murray, Roche, Cooney, Houlihan, Meade, Joy, Davis, McCue, Bruce, Healey, Sullivan, Foley, Fitzpatrick, Keats and Lynch.

As those family names indicate, the inhabitants of Argentia were of British origin, primarily Irish and English; hence the language spoken there was a mixture of Gaelic and English, which accounts for such words as "cauld" (cold), "auld" (old) and "bafe" (beef).

Those early settlers did not remain in Argentia during the whole year. In late autumn they crossed the harbour to a place called Placentia Sound, which was quite sheltered and more habitable than Argentia in the wintertime. In the Sound the men cut timber and logs, which they coasted back to Argentia in the spring to be used in the construction of houses, boats, stages and wharves. During their stay in the Sound the men also snared rabbits and caught trout; the women, in addition to their regular chores, carded and spun wool, which they used to knit mitts, socks, underwear and sweaters.

The staple food for the winter was a barrel of Injun (Indian) meal which was used instead of flour, and three or four barrels of salted herring. Up to this time there was no tea, so they boiled spruce boughs to make a drink they called "switchel." They lived in log houses called "tilts", with open fireplaces to provide heat and a means of cooking, which was done in a pot hanging by a hook over the open fire.

In the late 1820s an Englishman named Bouton established a business at Argentia, bringing several tradesmen with him. This accounts for at least some of our English ancestors; Smith, Hunt, and Hall are names originating in the southwest of England. Since the suffix "smith" at that time was attached to a person's particular trade—for example, blacksmith, tinsmith, goldsmith—it is probable that the original Smith was a tradesman who came over with Bouton. We know John Hall came from England and was a stonemason. In our Parish Register in Freshwater (which contains records transferred from the Argentia parish during the resettlement) it states that on February 19, 1838 he married a Charlotte Lambe of Red Island. The part of Argentia he settled in came to be known as Hall's Point.

Argentia Houses—
These photos were taken by the Americans just before they demolished the houses.

When the 1836 census was taken there were 76 dwelling houses in Argentia, with a population of 484 people. By this time several other business places had been established. Byrd's had a flourishing supply business located at the Pond Head. The Burkes were engaged in the fish trade. Robert Ledwell, who came from Ireland, also conducted an extensive fishing business at the Pond Head and owned several big schooners. Mr. Patrick Foran had a large general store in Sandy Cove. Around this time a post office was opened and John Burke was appointed the first postmaster.

Thus it is understandable that former residents experience a mixture of amusement and annoyance at people who are under the impression that Argentia was uninhabited up to the time of the construction of the Base. In fact, it was one of the most important and prosperous communities in Placentia Bay.

Tombstone of Rev. Pelagius Nowlan

In the old cemetery there were many tombstones that dated back to the 1700s. The oldest was that of Bryan Fitzpatrick.

The Lighthouse at Point Latine

In 1831 Father Pelagius Nowlan came from Ireland and founded a parish at Argentia. This was the first parish to be established in Placentia Bay, and it included the communities of Great Placentia, the Cape Shore, Fox Harbour, Ship Harbour and all Placentia Bay communities as far west as Oderin (the names found in the parish records prove this to be correct). In 1832 Father Nowlan erected the first school, which opened with an enrolment of 65 pupils. It was located under Power's Hill; a church was later built in the same location and was opened in 1836. Father Nowlan lived in Argentia for 40 years, died there in 1871 at the age of 84, and was buried in the cemetery nearby.

The community was actually known as *Little Placentia* until 1904, when Father John St. John, the parish priest at the time, had the name changed to *Argentia* after a silver mine nearby—"argent" being the French word for "silver."

Because Argentia extended over such a large area, different sections were given their own distinctive names—Point Moll, Marquise, Salmonier, Smith's Point, Traverse's Cove, Sandy Cove, Point Roche, Sampson's Point, Pond Head, Power's Hill and Point Latine. The latter was the site of a lighthouse erected for the benefit of the many fishing boats and steamers passing near that point of land. It is said to be named for a ship, the *Latine,* which was wrecked off the point. Its great light could be seen for many miles. The first lightkeeper was Patrick Foran, and the care of the lighthouse remained with the Foran family until the community was leased to the United States Government in 1941.

In 1916 the cornerstone of a new church was laid in a more central part of the community by Father John Ashley. A presbytery was also erected nearby, as well as a new school with three classrooms on the ground floor and a dance hall on the second. Both church and school were dedicated to the Rosary, hence the site came to be known as Mount Rosary, and the parish was called Holy Rosary Parish.

Point Latine Lighthouse, July 1942, after the the construction of Argentia Naval Station began

When the new church was completed the bell was removed from the former one and placed in a belfry, and was rung from the choir. It had been installed in the old church in 1901 by Father St. John, and was one of the finest in Newfoundland, weighing about two thousand pounds and costing $550, an enormous sum at that time. It had been made by the Henry McShane Foundry in Baltimore, Maryland. It now stands in the yard of Holy Rosary Church in Freshwater.

The Presbytery

Holy Rosary Church, Argentia

## Chapter Two

# EMPLOYMENT IN THE EARLY YEARS

Photo courtesyy Dept. Mines & Energy

A miner digging into the ore bed

Photo courtesy Placentia Area Historical Society

Argentia fishermen at the turn of the century

### The Mine

ARGENTIA WAS ONE OF SEVERAL NEWFOUNDLAND MINE SITES named after their specific mineral deposits. This silver lode was discovered by a John Burke of Argentia. Because of financial difficulties he could not develop his claim, and so had to sell it to Baron Francis Von Ellershausen, a German engineer who came to Canada in 1862 to develop the copper mine in Bett's Cove, Notre Dame Bay. In 1883, under a London firm called the Cliff Silver Mines Company, Ellerhausen began working at Silver Cliff, as the Argentia mine came to be known. He found it in bad shape due to the previous unskilled mining efforts, and he left Newfoundland the following year. Several other attempts were made to promote Silver Cliff, but they were unsuccessful. In 1887 a shipment of ore bound for Britain sank in the mid-Atlantic. St. John's merchant and auctioneer John W. Foran obtained the property in 1892 and finally located the main orebody, which the others had not been able to find; in spite of this, he made no profit.

The last attempt was carried out between 1922 and 1925 by the Silver Cliff Mining Company of St. John's, but it met with no greater success than had the preceding efforts. Since 1941 the mine has been part of the territory under the jurisdiction of the U.S. Naval Base.

It is impossible now to ascertain how much employment was created locally by the working of this mine, but it is definite that during the last phase of its operation men from Argentia were employed.

### The Fishery

The codfishery was the mainstay of the economy of Argentia during the 19th century. Large boats called *bankers*, with crews of 10 to 15 men, fished on the Grand Banks. Smaller boats with crews of 5 or 6 fished at Golden Bay near Cape St. Mary's. The inshore fishery was operated from small open boats which returned home daily.

Since there was no refrigeration the fish had to be split, salted, and dried on rough platforms called *flakes*. The livers of the

A typical banking schooner, one of many which fished Newfoundland's Grand Banks

codfish were put in a pork barrel and allowed to rot. The oil produced from the rotting livers was used for nutritional purposes and also to provide light by means of the cod oil lamp, the only source of artificial light at the time. A string of wool soaked in the cod oil served as a wick. (The kerosene lamp came into use at a later date, and we did not have the luxury of electricity until 1925.)

The fishermen saw very little cash for their labour. In the spring the fish merchants advanced whatever materials, gear and food would be needed for the season, and at the end of the season they bought the fish, deducted what was owed to them, and paid the fishermen the balance "in kind" with flour, pork, salt beef and molasses. By the end of February these staple foods would be almost used up, which accounts for the expression "the long, hungry month of March".

Then, as now, the price of fish fluctuated from year to year, and of course a good catch could never be a certainty. By the late 1800s the Bank fishery at Argentia had ended. The next generation of young men had begun emigrating to the U.S. in search of steadier and more lucrative employment.

## THE LIQUOR TRADE

In the early 1920s liquor was not easily obtained legally, and at one time it was even necessary to get a prescription from a doctor. Later a permit could be purchased which allowed the owner to buy two bottles a week. Because of those restrictions there was a brisk trade in liquor brought from St. Pierre to Argentia. The fishing captains who dealt in this illegal trade had their regular customers, some of whom retailed it while others shipped it on to St. John's. There is a story told of one wholesaler who sank his stock in a pond while waiting to dispose of it. He had apparently been watched by some young men who, under cover of darkness, stole the entire stock.

*The extension of the railway to Argentia brought mixed feelings, as illustrated in the following poem. It was composed by Professor William Murphy, who returned to Argentia in the 1920s to find the railway terminal built on his homestead.*

As I stood on this mountain top
Just twenty years ago
I stood and watched the sun go down
In a thousand-tinted glow.

I see the fleet of fishing boats,
Full many a moving speck.
I see the waves that gently break
On distant Marquise Neck.

The Reach, Point Moll and Latine
Are all beneath my eyes.
No scene of beauty like to this
I've seen in foreign skies.

What is that ugly creeping thing
Right where the house should be?
I guess the wheels of progress
Have been making sport of me.

The engine fires are burning now
Right where our hearth fire glowed.
The sleepers have replaced the bed
My mother fondly sowed.

Progress marches onwards,
And though my heart is sad,
I've delved into the future
And I cannot but be glad.

For the needs of future people
Often call for sorrow now.
My mead to those who follow
I must cheerfully allow.

All ye whose dreams and
thoughts of home
Are tinged in a foreign land,
Come back betimes and visit it
While still the old home stands.

For you cannot know the heartache,
Or the bitter longing tell,
When only "memory" is left
Of the home you loved so well.

There were a few retailers, or *bootleggers*, as they were called, who continued their trade even after the construction of the U.S. Naval Base began. Restrictions were lifted, however, and liquor permits discontinued at the time of "Come Home Year" in 1966.

## TRANSPORTATION

Until 1920 the terminus of the Placentia branch of the railway had been at Jersey Side. There was, however, no safe harbour for the coastal boats which took passengers and freight to their final destinations around Placentia Bay and along the South Coast as far as Port-aux-Basques. It was decided then to extend the railway to Argentia, which had a safe, landlocked harbour, for the most part ice-free in winter. Of course this did not sit well with the people of Placentia, who aired their opposition in the press in no uncertain terms; nevertheless, the change was made. It is worth noting that on its first run to the new Argentia terminus the freight consisted of the pews for the newly erected Church on Mount Rosary; these are the same pews now being used in the Holy Rosary Church in Freshwater.

The extension of the railway to Argentia was a considerable boost to the economy of the community and probably accounts for the phasing out of the fishery there (with the exception of a few men at Pond Head who still engaged in the shore fishery). In addition to the construction of the line itself, there was employment for several longshoremen who transferred the freight from the train to the two coastal boats, the *Argyle* and the *Glencoe*; these boats made regular runs to and from Argentia. The Railway station itself gave employment to a number of people: the station agent, George Abbott; the assistant, Abbott's son Walter; telegraph operator/dispatcher Raymond Whelan; customs collector Matt Murphy; and tidewaiter Albert O'Reilly. As well, several Argentia men secured positions on the train and on the coastal boats, while some crew members from outside the com-

Freight train arriving at Argentia

Phoro courtesy Placentia Area Historical Society

munity rented houses and took up residence in Argentia with their families.

The passenger train to Argentia made its last run in 1983, ending 63 years of service.

About twice a year coal boats arrived and had to be unloaded manually, thus employing many extra workers, even if only for a short time. Those working in the hold of the ship shovelled the coal into large tubs which were then hoisted by crane. This coal was used to generate steam for the engines of the train and for the steamers.

To accommodate passengers coming and going on the coastal boats, the Davis Hotel was built soon after Argentia became the terminus. This provided a few more jobs. Obviously then, the railway had an impact on the community from both a social and an economic point of view.

## HEALTH CARE

Because the Commission of Government—which replaced Responsible Government in 1934—was concerned with the health care of the people, thirteen small "cottage hospitals" were located throughout the island. One was built at Argentia in 1936 to serve not only the residents of the immediate area but also people living in the small and remote communities of Placentia Bay. The hospital was erected quite near the dock for the convenience of those patients who came by way of coastal boats. The resident physician, a Dr. John Green from Toronto, was well liked and gave excellent medical service. The hospital provided some employment in addition to filling a great need in the life of the whole area.

Argentia Cottage Hospital

## THE HERRING FACTORY

In 1936 a herring factory was built near the site of the present C.N. Terminal. Fishermen from around Placentia Bay brought their catches to this factory, where they were dried in a rotary drier operated by steam power. The herring was then ground into fish meal and exported for poultry feed. Although this was only a seasonal operation it provided some badly needed employment, since by now we were feeling the effects of the dreadful Depression of 1929-1939.

## Chapter Three

# TRANSPORTATION

**B**ECAUSE A STRETCH OF WATER CALLED THE PLACENTIA GUT separated Jersey Side from Placentia, the only road connecting Argentia with communities outside the area was a very poor one along the shore of North East Arm to Dunville, and this road ended at the head of the Arm. Except for the train we were virtually on an island. The government provided a regular crossing of the Placentia Gut by motor boat. The boat crossed at fifteen-minute intervals from early morning until midnight, but the service was often interrupted by wind and winter ice conditions. It was discontinued altogether during the retrenchment carried out by the Commission of Government during the Depression.

To travel to St. John's from Argentia by car was quite an undertaking. Having negotiated the rough road from Argentia to the Placentia Gut, the driver would have to hire two motor boats which would then be lashed together. The car would be driven down two planks, the front wheels placed in one boat and the rear wheels in the other. On reaching the Placentia side the car would be driven up the two planks. The driver then faced a trip of at least three hours over a very poor, narrow road.

Rev. Fr. Adrian Dee crossing Placentia Gut, *circa* 1927

Father Adrian Dee, who became our parish priest in 1922, was the owner of the first car in Argentia. A few years later other cars appeared on the scene, but it was not until 1942 that a scow was placed on the Placentia Gut by the Americans to transport vehicles (for travel to the wireless stations they had set up on the Cape Shore). They later replaced this with a pontoon bridge, but because of the strong tides the bridge could not be kept in place. The fate of the bridge told in the following ballad, composed by some local residents:

THE BRIDGE AT PLACENTIA GUT

In my erstwhile cogitations, I could never fathom why
Placentia's sons were famous at the good old "do or die"
I think I've solved the riddle, and it isn't "sisu* but"
The fighter instinct nurtured, in years crossing o'er the gut.

As I sit in Murphy's window, watching Kelly o'er the way
Chin-waggin' with the Yankees,(I hope he makes them pay)
I could read a good detective, had I brought a book along,
Those darn beer-laden Yankees must be near a hundred strong.

The Yankees with their notions, put a bridge from shore to shore
Which was just the merest trifle of what they really had in store
For the benighted Newfies, but their reckonings were bad
'Cause what happened to the pontoon bridge was really very sad.

"You'll never do it, Mister," said old-timer on the beach
And he knew more than Harvard, or what Boston U. could teach.
"Man and boy, I've been crossing o'er that gut for fifty years,
And the bridge will be a failure,'spite the Yanks' gold,
sweat and tears."

"Manila ropes won't hold that bridge", said Skipper Tom who knew,
"Why a western moored at Golden Bay, would snap those
ropes in two
Those killicks made from cement blocks won't hold that bridge I say
You'll be climbing the Devil's Bit next week, to see it in Herring Bay."

But the Yankees were independent, and they laughed the
Newfies down
And ridiculed opinions from the wisest in the Town,
In weather fair and beautiful, they put the bridge in place
And when finished celebrated, drinking whiskey by the case.

One day it blew from the Nor' Nor' West, and it blew a livin' gale
The Yankees donned their parka hoods, the Chink on the
beach grew pale,
The Maintenance Crew on the bridge looked blue, 'twas old-timer's
turn to laugh
As he saw the Yank Engineer's great feat float up the arm like a raft.

* "sisu" is probably a poetic abbreviation of sisyphean – everlasting labour – referring to Sisyphus in Greek mythology. (Source: The Concise Oxford Dictionary).

When it came abreast the islands, Tom Barron rang the "alert"
"Tis a sub," said he, "To the shelters, or someone's sure to get hurt."
John Hartley ran to scuttle his boat, Kate Barron burned the mail,
Some more set forth to the Railway shed, while more looked
o'er the rail.

" 'Tis a Nazi sub," said Henry Hunt, "and not those wily Japs,"
(He reads the Family Herald, and studies the war from maps)
"The Japs would take the islands, but they're coming along this way,
They'll shell Greg Power's plant for sure, on their way to
Herring Bay."

Well, the "ALL CLEAR" sounded early, 'cause Tom Collins
from the Head
Came to Dunville for the kerosene, before he went to bed
"I know you'll say I'm drinking," as he slowly shook his head
"There's a bridge on the North East River," were the
very words he said.

So, if you're coming to Placentia, and you're very welcome, mind
You will not see those pontoons, but you'll see what's left behind
It's a kind of ramp or breakwater, a-jutting out from shore
Just stand on that, and then do this, — cup your hands and R O A R

And if Kelly does not hear you, push a dory off the beach
And row, me boys, with all your might, to get across the reach
You may land up in Dunville, and you'll swear a little but
You'll know just why the Yankees failed to bridge Placentia Gut.

Pontoon Bridge on Placentia Gut, 1941

The Americans then built a road through Dunville that connected with the route to Colinet and on to St. John's. This road, completed in 1943, was a military necessity for the Americans and a great convenience for the travelling public.

In the meantime, the Kelly Brothers of Jersey Side continued to operate a motor boat on the Gut until 1954, when the *Sir Ambrose Shea* was put into service by the Liberal Government. This motor ferry was capable of carrying several cars, as well as passengers, for a small fee. The service continued until the present bridge—the Sir Ambrose Shea Highway Lift Bridge—was completed in 1961. Although the centre span weighs 100 tons it can be raised in 1½ minutes. A lift bridge was necessary because of the many fishing boats and other craft leaving and entering the two Arms—the North East Arm and the South East Arm. It was supposed to be a toll bridge but Premier Joseph R. Smallwood, ever mindful of votes in the next election, announced in his speech on the occasion of the formal opening that it would be toll-free.

The Motor Ferry *Sir Ambrose Shea*

This bridge has brought about a great change in the social life of the area, especially for the youth, some of whom now come from neighbouring communities to attend the high school and community college at Placentia. People have access to social and athletic activities in other towns, and may now easily drive to their place of employment. It has certainly been a great boon to the travelling public and the business community.

In 1979 the Argentia Access Road to the Trans-Canada Highway was finished, and so at last our isolation was completely ended and we had a modern road link with the outside world.

The Sir Ambrose Shea Lift Bridge, Placentia, opened October 28, 1961

This information was handed out at the Official Opening Ceremony

THE SIR AMBROSE SHEA LIFT BRIDGE

The Sir Ambrose Shea Lift Bridge consists of two approach spans and one centre vertical lift span each 100 feet in length. The total weight of the centre span which can be raised in one and a half minutes is 100 tons. Clearance under the span in the down position is 10 feet, and, when raised 70 feet.

Work on the Bridge commenced on August 29, 1959 and by December 1960 the abutments, piers and approach spans had been completed. Winter and the abnormal ice conditions of the Spring of 1961, delayed resumption of work until May 1961, when the first shipment of steel for the centre span arrived at the site.

Every precaution has been taken to ensure safety when the lift span is in operation including the installation of gates and lights at both approaches; and cross controls ensuring that the centre span cannot be lifted until the gates are closed.

Foundation of Canada Engineering Corporation Limited designed and supervised construction with McNamara Construction acting as the main contractors. Subcontracts for erection of the steel, installing mechanical gear and electrical controls were held by Ocean Steel and Construction, Link-Belt, Limited; and Canadian Comstock Limited.

*Programme*

CHAIRMAN
Hon. F.W. Rowe, B.A., B.Paed., D.Paed., M.H.A.
Minister of Highways

Ode to Newfoundland

INVOCATION
Reverend Father J. Hunt, P.P.

GREETINGS
Mr. Leonard Miller
Mayor of Placentia

Hon. G.A. Frecker, B.A., B.E., D.Paed., LL.D., M.H.A.
Minister of Education and Representative for the District

ADDRESS AND FORMAL OPENING CEREMONY
Hon. J.R. Smallwood, D.C.L., LL.D., D.Litt., M.H.A.

The National Anthem

Format of the Official Opening Programme

## Chapter Four

# THE PEOPLE OF ARGENTIA

THE PENINSULA OF ARGENTIA WAS CONNECTED TO THE MAINLAND mass by a very narrow neck of land called Marquise Neck. The name "Marquise" is most likely connected with the presence of the French in Placentia in the 17th century. The sub-community of Marquise had its own two-room school, Post Office, and two general stores. In the early 1920s it had about 35 families and a school population of around 60. Marquise and the Argentia Peninsula, together with the smaller outlying settlements, made up the sprawling community known as Argentia.

Too much praise cannot be given to the people of Argentia who, like their ancestors, were hard-working, industrious and independent. Most of the male population found gainful employment at home, and those who were not so fortunate sought work elsewhere. Because many of them were carpenters, they built their own homes and kept them in good repair. They supplemented their income by cultivating hayfields, growing a variety of vegetables, and raising livestock and poultry. The women were thrifty, sewing or knitting most of the articles of clothing needed by their families; they also helped with the gardening and the haymaking. Consequently during the ten years of the Depression very few Argentia people had to seek government assistance.

Map of Argentia. The top portion is the Argentia Peninsula; the bottom portion is Marquise and a number of smaller settlements.

There existed a good spirit of neighbourliness and Christian charity, and one could always depend on the help of others in times of difficulty; this was especially so when illness or death occurred in a family. Should someone be seriously ill, neighbours would volunteer in turn to stay up with the patient all night. Since there were no funeral parlours, the deceased was waked at home. Again, neighbours volunteered to be present all throughout the night at the wake; this custom was true to our Irish heritage. A carpenter would build, cover and line the coffin while several young men would dig the grave; all this was done willingly and without any thought of payment.

Because none of the homes had telephones (with the exception of Father Dee's and a pay phone for general use) the people visited each other often and a warm reception and friendly chat could always be assured. They were intelligent people who kept abreast of current affairs, both local and foreign, even before the advent of radio. As parents they were keenly interested in education, and it is to their credit that so many of their children entered the teaching and nursing professions as well as careers in the business world.

Of course there were numerous social activities. The annual Garden Party, always held on August 15, was the greatest festivity of the year. It took place in a large field not far from where the C N Ferry Dock is now. Suppers and refreshments were to be had, as well as sideshows and games of chance. The great majority of the community attended, and people came by boat from Fox Harbour as well. On a couple of occasions the train went to Jersey Side to accommodate those from the Placentia area who wished to attend. The highlight of the Garden Party was an impromptu concert that night in the Parish Hall, followed by a dance which lasted until broad daylight.

There was usually a Ball on Easter Monday night, where the ladies wore formal gowns and the Belle of the Ball was decided by vote. Quadrilles, lancers and waltzes were danced to the lively music of the accordion. About midnight a generous

meal was served in the dining area. Of course there was no bar service at that time. Gentlemen so inclined, however, brought along a flask which they shared with their friends, but not in the dance hall. At that time rum was the usual drink, taken "straight", and on an occasion like that, straight from the bottle.

At the end of the first school term each year a concert was held, followed by a presentation of prizes and awards won during the previous year. St. Patrick's night never passed without an Irish concert, and I must add, there was never any scarcity of local talent.

To raise funds for some particular cause, card parties were held in the Parish Hall or in private homes. Card-playing was the chief pastime of families then, since there was neither radio nor television. With a couple of neighbours and a small "kitty" the night passed all too quickly. Bingo was unheard of at that time.

Argentia was always a peaceful community; the Church was the focus of the lives of the people. Their leader and counsellor was the parish priest, to whom they always showed the greatest respect and gave their wholehearted co-operation. Criminal acts, even those of a minor nature, were almost unheard of.

Unfortunately, this peace and tranquillity was to be brought to an abrupt end with the outbreak of World War II.

## Chapter Five

# OUTBREAK OF WORLD WAR II

ALTHOUGH WORLD WAR I WAS SUPPOSED TO BE "THE WAR TO END all wars," this did not prove to be so. In fact, the world was led into the greatest conflict of all time. Germany had suffered a crushing defeat in 1914 and was made to sign the Peace Treaty of Versailles, by which she was allowed only enough troops and armaments to protect her own territory; as well, she had to pay huge reparations in money and goods to her conquerors. Consequently the Germans were angry and resentful, their Emperor had fled, and there was widespread unemployment, inflation and poverty.

Out of nowhere, it seemed, appeared an agitator and fanatic named Adolf Hitler. With his frenzied oratory he held the German people spellbound with promises of employment and with the idea that they were a master race.

The employment turned out to be the manufacturing of armaments in preparation for war, and the people willingly accepted

Fleet of ships in Argentia Harbour

Photo courtesy Placentia Area Historical Society

such slogans as "guns for butter" as they blindly followed Hitler's commands. Great super highways were built by forced labour. German youth were enroled in the Hitler Youth Organization, not realizing they were being trained for war.

With his country now well prepared, Hitler soon broke the peace treaty and began invading country after country in Europe. He knew that Great Britain desired peace at all costs, since she was certainly unready for war. The invasion of Poland, however, was the last straw and on September 3, 1939 France joined Britain in declaring war on Germany. On that day when the news was announced to the world, who would have thought life would soon changed so drastically for the people of Argentia?

The United States gave supplies of all varieties to Britain; American ships were not to transport the cargoes, however, for fear the Germans would sink one of them, thus bringing the U.S. into the war. President Franklin D. Roosevelt realized that Britain had to ensure her vital supplies from this side of the Atlantic would get through the German U-Boat-infested waters; if they could not, the Germans would conquer the Allies, cross the ocean and invade America. Because so many valuable cargoes were being lost, the U.S. decided to give Britain 50 destroyers to help safeguard the cargo ships, and the U.S. was granted territory to establish bases in British North America.

Robert Conway, Staff Correspondent of the New York *News*, said there were published reports at the time that British Prime Minister Winston Churchill offered all of Newfoundland to the U.S. when the destroyer deal was negotiated, and that Roosevelt replied: "Winston, you can't sell your bankrupt territories to us to look after".

Since Newfoundland is the stepping stone to Europe from continental North America, or—as we learned in our Geography at school—the nearest part of the new world to the old, it was the ideal strategic point for U.S. bases. Soon we began hearing rumours that Argentia would be the most likely choice. Since we were still suffering the effects of the Great Depression of the thirties, our first reaction was to anticipate the employment that the construction of the Base would create. Little did we think that our whole community, both living and dead, would be uprooted and moved to another location.

In looking back and realizing what the requirements were for a great naval base, it is quite obvious that Argentia was the ideal choice. The land was flat and therefore suitable for runways, it had an ice-free deep-water harbour and it was a railway terminus. Argentia was destined to play a major role in the execution of World War II by the allies.

The German U-Boats were moving farther and farther into the North Atlantic and had established weather stations in Greenland. So in December 1940 the Commission of Government—which consisted of a British Governor, three British

Commissioners, and three Newfoundland Commissioners—enacted the Defence (Requisition of Land) Regulations, authorizing the compulsory acquisition of private property for the purpose of constructing U.S. military bases in Newfoundland. The following document details the Regulations:

> In exercise of the powers conferred upon me by the Defence (requisition of land) Regulations, made under the Emergency Powers Defence Act 1940, on the 28th day of December, A.D., 1940, I do authorize all persons who shall be engaged by the United States Government or its agents or contractors on the construction for that government of any naval, military, or air works at Argentia to do any work on any land or place any thing in, on, or over any land upon the Argentia Peninsula, in so far as it shall be necessary for any such person so to do for the carrying out of any such work of construction including any preliminary work in relation thereto.
>
> Provided, however, that this present authority shall not be valid to authorize the demolition, pulling down, or destruction of any building or erection upon any such land, or the doing of any act which renders any such building or erection intangible.
>
> Signed,
> Wilfrid Woods
> Commissioner for Public Utilities

Rumour had now become fact, and people grew more and more disturbed as they realized that they would be uprooted from their homes. Twenty-four householders in Pond Head received notice early in the winter that they would have to vacate almost immediately. As a result, two meetings of all householders were held in January. A detailed account of these meetings is given below.

> Because of general uneasiness and anxiety, and at public request, a general meeting of all householders of the settlement of Argentia was convened, and held on January 1st, 1941. A committee to represent the whole people was elected as follows:
>
> E. P. Houlihan, Chairman
> D. O'Reilly, Secretary
> T. F. Kelly
> P. Kelly
> A. Bruce

It was decided that a lawyer should be retained to advise, and if possible, represent.

During the discussion, it was felt that very short notice had been given to twenty-four householders, to leave their homes; that the month of January, more especially after a severe epidemic of influenza is unsuitable for moving, unless houses that are suitable are prepared temporarily at some central point, that will also be near the work; Houses at a distance of three or four miles that may not have been occupied for years, are not considered suitable.

Provisions for cattle, fodder, fuel, etc., should be made.

People should not be asked to leave their homes, until they have a definite guarantee of the quality and amount of recompense; that a Board of Arbitration sit at Argentia, on which, at least two members represent the people of Argentia.

At a second general meeting held in Argentia on January 2nd, 1941, presided over by the Chairman of the Committee, the following resolutions were read and adopted unanimously.

> BE IT RESOLVED: That the people of Argentia look with anxiety on any plan that would include moving people in the winter, unless suitable provisions be made for people and property at some place within or near the settlement of Argentia.
>
> SECONDLY, That it is our wish that a Board of Arbitration, two members of which would represent the people of Argentia, should sit at Argentia before anyone be asked to move.
>
> THIRDLY, That a definite guarantee of the type of recompense be given in writing by this Board, before the people be asked to move.
>
> FOURTHLY, That suitable provision be made for work for the people of the vicinity, first, before any others be considered.
>
> FIFTHLY, That special provision be made for the aged and the sick.
>
> SIXTHLY, That when a permanent settlement of the people of Argentia and vicinity be planned, a town site shall be chosen convenient to all, that they shall live together in one town, with their own Parish Church and Schools, as at present constituted.
>
> BE IT FURTHER RESOLVED ALSO: That a copy of this memorial be sent to
>
> His Excellency the Governor, Sir Humphrey Walwyn,
>
> His Grace, Most Reverend E.P. Roche, Archbishop of St. John's,
>
> The Honourable Commissioner for Justice and Defence,
>
> The Honourable Commissioner for Natural Resources,
>
> The Honourable Commissioner for Public Utilities,
>
> The Chief Officer in Newfoundland in charge of American Defence.
>
> Secretary.
> Argentia,
> Jan. 2nd 1941.

Photo courtesy Dr. John Lewis

Phillip J. Lewis, L.LB.

Philip J. Lewis, L.LB. of the firm of Barron and Lewis was retained by the Argentia Committee to act on behalf of the people who would have to be resettled.

## Chapter Six

# RESETTLEMENT

The story is told that early residents of Argentia used to see at times, perhaps with certain weather conditions, what appeared to be a flag raised on a staff. They believed it to be a bad omen—the sign of an impending storm. That location on the North side of Argentia, in fact, came to be known by the residents as The Flagstaff. It is rather ironic that about a century later the American flag was raised in approximately the same area. (This story was told to Mrs. Molly Power, a former Argentia resident, by her mother.) The storm eventually turned up—in 1941.

ON FEBRUARY 13, 1941 THE AMERICAN FLAG WAS RAISED IN Argentia and the people felt like foreigners in their own community.

Living conditions soon became rather uncomfortable for many families as runways and trenches for water, sewer lines and underground cables were constructed on or near their property. The people became more disturbed as construction activity increased, and with it the realization that very soon they would have to vacate their homes. These were the homes they themselves had built, the homes into which they had brought their brides, where their children had been born and raised, and where they had expected to live out their lives. Their land had been developed through several generations and was an important part of their livelihood. It was especially traumatic for the elderly to realize they would have to tear up their roots and start life over again—where, they did not know.

Even though there was a national emergency, provision for the permanent resettlement of the people should have been made before construction of the Base began. The Commission of Government, as guardian of the people's rights, safety and security, could have and should have made the necessary arrangements in advance. At the time money was flowing like water. Millions upon millions were spent under a cost-plus contract; the Base eventually cost $52,000,000—a tremendous amount of money in 1941. If the people of Argentia had dealt directly with the U.S. Government, would not a town with modern conveniences have been built for them in the beginning? The Americans were a generous and understanding people; they must have sympathized with the plight of those who had been forced to leave their homes and their community at a time when they had no elected voice to represent them.

On January 31 Wilfrid W. Woods, the Commissioner for Public Utilities, informed Mr. Philip Lewis that the Americans had now requested 57 families to be moved immediately. He also said that he opposed their building houses in Marquise, since that community was to be evacuated itself in a few months. After lengthy discussion with Mr. Lewis, however, he reluctantly agreed that the families could move to Marquise as a temporary arrangement. They had to sell their livestock and, taking with them only their household possessions, move into vacant houses, some of which had been unoccupied for years. A few families were given shelter by relatives or friends.

The following item appeared in the St. John's newspaper *The Daily News* around that time:

> The position is one that should never have occurred. It has been due only to the inadequacy of the preparations made by the Government to meet a new and difficult situation. For months it has been known that there would be an American base in Argentia. For months it has been known that the property of most of the people would be expropriated. But no one went down to talk to the people and advise them and little has followed the delayed visit of representatives of the Commission to the district. It goes without saying that a situation of this kind could not have occurred in pre-Commission times. Now that we are supposed to have an efficient administration, why has it been allowed to occur?

The Americans at first burned the homes as an efficient way of demolishing them. However, this was so traumatic on the residents that many objections were voiced, and finally the burnings stopped and they bulldozed the rest.

Resettlement meant not only the moving of the people and the demolition of their homes; also to be considered were the church building, presbytery, hall, two school buildings and a club. When the U.S. Navy served notice that by May 1 they would require the area occupied by the buildings on Mount Rosary, Father Dee made plans to build a temporary church, presbytery and school in Marquise. When he was informed in April that construction of the Army Base was to begin there in a few months, he was greatly disappointed. His earnest desire was to keep his parish intact.

The people were becoming impatient to be re-established permanently without further delay, and on April 6 they held another public meeting. They now wished to be resettled in the North East Arm of Dunville in an area known as Herring Bay, where they believed the soil to be suitable for agriculture and they could once again supplement their incomes. They were willing to finance the building of their homes, but wanted the Government to carry out the necessary survey work. Below are the resolutions that were drawn up and sent to the Commission of Government.

> WHEREAS, we the people of Argentia, in Public Meeting convened, on this, Sunday, the sixth day of April, A.D. 1941, have resolved to forward to His Majesty's Commission of Government the subjoined Resolutions, relative to the resettlement of the People of this Community, who have been, and are about to be, dispossessed, because of the requisitioning of our homes and property by the government of Newfoundland; and
>
> WHEREAS it is expedient and necessary that steps be taken by the Government of Newfoundland, forthwith, to make preliminary arrangements for our re-establishment

WHEREAS, we are desirous of being re-settled in a new Community with the utmost dispatch, and before the next winter season arrives: and

WHEREAS, we, the undersigned are unanimously in favour of being resettled in the North-east Arm of Placentia, and in the vicinity of the locality known as Herring Bay; and

WHEREAS, we are prepared to finance the erection of our own homes in the said area, but we realize that certain preliminary steps must be taken by the Government, before our intentions in this respect will materialize.

BE IT RESOLVED that His Majesty's Government be requested to instruct its proper Departmental officers to make immediate arrangements for the sending to the N.E. Arm of Placentia, and particularly to that section, known as Herring Bay, a properly equipped, fully qualified, and competent party of surveyors to examine the locality for the purpose of ascertaining its suitability for the establishment of a Settlement at that place, and particularly, to examine the soil from the standpoint of its agricultural possibilities, as well as the area available for such purposes.

BE IT FURTHER RESOLVED, that the said party of surveyors be instructed to survey the said area for the purpose of ascertaining its suitability as a township site;

And, BE IT FURTHER RESOLVED, that the said surveyors be qualified to conduct a competent survey for the laying out of road communications between the said proposed site, and Argentia Peninsula, and that they be instructed to do so.

BE IT FURTHER RESOLVED, that should the said surveys establish the suitability of such an area for the purpose required, that the Government express its willingness to make available for the clearing of the said land such mechanical equipment, and agricultural machinery, as it may have at its disposal for the expediting of the work in hand. It is also requested that the Government express its willingness to make available such of its agricultural and engineering staffs, as may be requisite and necessary for the laying out of the said township, and for the instruction and guidance of the people, in the establishment of their agricultural holdings.

BE IT FURTHER RESOLVED, that it is the unanimous desire of this meeting that such Departmental officers as may be detailed for the carrying out of the foregoing scheme of resettlement, shall work in close co-operation with the Committee which the people of this Community propose to appoint, for the purpose of piloting this plan of resettlement.

SIGNED AT ARGENTIA, THIS 6th DAY OF APRIL, A.D. 1941, by the UNDERSIGNED RESIDENTS OF ARGENTIA WHOSE PROPERTIES ARE BEING EXPROPRIATED.

On April 15 a favourable reply was received from W. W. Woods informing the Resettlement Committee; a survey party and an Agricultural Officer would proceed to Herring Bay as soon as possible, and the survey for a road to Argentia would be undertaken. Woods further stated that the people of Argentia could rely on the sympathy of the government, which would give them all the assistance necessary to resettle themselves in their new community.

On May 3 these assurances were repeated in a letter from Mr. Howell, Secretary for Agriculture and Rural Reconstruction, along with the information that a survey of Herring Bay would begin on May 7 and that in a short while the plans for the layout of the town would be available. However, at the beginning of June Father Dee visited the site with officials from the Department of Natural Resources, and was convinced at that time that Herring Bay would be unsuitable for the new settlement. This was quite a setback, especially for those who had already left their homes and were living in temporary quarters. On June 13 Father Dee proposed Freshwater as the new town site.

The priest's frustration must have reached boiling point on July 7 when he wrote the following letter to the Officer in Charge at Argentia:

July 7, 1941

Lieutenant J. Silliman,
Officer in Charge,
Naval Air Station,
Argentia.

Dear Sir,

Since January last, the people of Argentia have shown their willingness to co-operate with the work of the United States Government in the construction of the Naval Base here at Argentia. Now, because of the procrastination of our local Government in arranging for their rehabilitation, and because of the working of the Leasing of Bases Agreement, that people need not leave their homes, until at least temporary habitation has been supplied for the people. The people of Argentia and Marquise, acting under my advice, which the delayed action of our Government has forced me to give, will not move from their present homes, until such facilities as roads, and cleared ground, make it possible for them to build homes in a new Settlement. For the site of this Settlement, they have chosen the area between the boundary of the American Territory and the Jersey Side, Placentia.

I am taking full and personal responsibility for this action. I regret very much that it may seem obstructive to your very important work, but because the original people of this Parish are my main interest, I can take no other course.

May I suggest, Sir, that because of the short time before the approach of winter, and the seriousness of this matter which apparently does

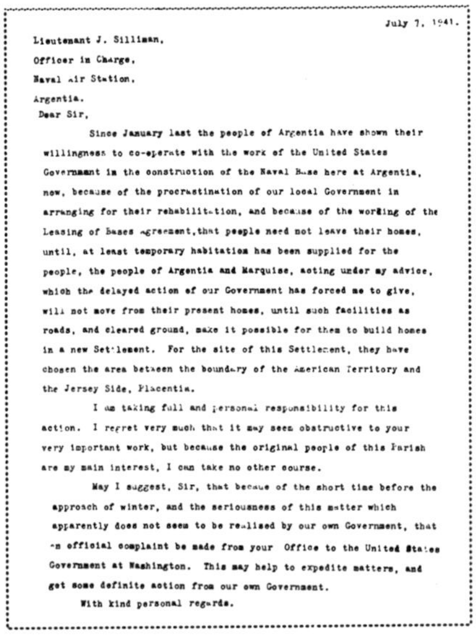
July 7, 1941.

Lieutenant J. Silliman,
Officer in Charge,
Naval Air Station,
Argentia.
Dear Sir,

Since January last the people of Argentia have shown their willingness to co-operate with the work of the United States Government in the construction of the Naval Base here at Argentia, now, because of the procrastination of our local Government in arranging for their rehabilitation, and because of the working of the Leasing of Bases Agreement, that people need not leave their homes, until, at least temporary habitation has been supplied for the people, the people of Argentia and Marquise, acting under my advice, which the delayed action of our Government has forced me to give, will not move from their present homes, until such facilities as roads, and cleared ground, make it possible for them to build homes in a new Settlement. For the site of this Settlement, they have chosen the area between the boundary of the American Territory and the Jersey Side, Placentia.

I am taking full and personal responsibility for this action. I regret very much that it may seem obstructive to your very important work, but because the original people of this Parish are my main interest, I can take no other course.

May I suggest, Sir, that because of the short time before the approach of winter, and the seriousness of this matter which apparently does not seem to be realised by our own Government, that an official complaint be made from your Office to the United States Government at Washington. This may help to expedite matters, and get some definite action from our own Government.

With kind personal regards.

Father Adrian J. Dee, Parish Priest in Argentia & Freshwater

not seem to be realised by our own Government, that an official complaint be made from your Office to the United States Government at Washington. This may help to expedite matters, and get some definite action from our own Government.

With kind personal regards.
I am,
Truly yours,
Rev. A. J. Dee
Parish Priest

This prompted Lieutenant Silliman to write the following letter two days later:

9th July, 1941

The Honourable Sir Wilfrid W. Woods,
Commissioner for Public Utilities,
Department of Public Works,
St. John's, Newfoundland

Dear Sir,

Further reference is made to my letters of June 24th and July 2nd concerning the removal of the remaining Argentia residents. It is not felt necessary to emphasize again the urgent necessity for completing the evacuation of the remaining residents in the shortest possible time, and it is understood that your Department feels that this evacuation can be completed by July 15th, 1941.

For your further information, a copy of a letter dated July 7th, 1941, received from Father Dee is enclosed. Father Dee handed this letter to me personally in order to explain why he was taking this present course of action. I pointed out, during the conversation, that regardless of our mutual friendship and personal humanitarian feelings, I would be forced to insist that every effort be made to complete the removal of the Argentia residents in accordance with the plan which has been operating for several months.

I understood from Mr. Sparks, local resettlement administrator, that temporary habitation has been arranged for the remaining residents, and that the implication in paragraph 1 of Father Dee's letter, that temporary accommodations are not available, may be in error.

I further understood from Father Dee that the completion of the survey for the proposed settlement site, including the preparation of a plot showing road locations, would considerably ease his present worries; and that your early agreement to assist promptly in the development of this site to the end that permanent resettlement may be accomplished in advance of the coming winter would completely eliminate his present objections. This verbal understanding varies somewhat from paragraph 1 of the enclosed letter, which states that Father Dee will not approve further evacuation of Argentia residents until the resettlement site has actually been prepared. This information is being given, since it may be of some possible assistance in promoting further co-operation between your Department and the interested parties in Argentia, to the end that the final steps toward the removal of the remaining residents may be accomplished in the shortest practicable time.

It would be greatly appreciated if you would advise me promptly if any developments occur which would further delay the resettlement program, in order that all necessary steps may be taken here to speed up the complete removal of the remaining residents.

Yours faithfully,
(Sgd) J. W.SILLIMAN,
Lieutenant (j.g.) CEC-V(S)
Resident Officer in Charge

Copies of Father Dee's and Lieutenant Silliman's correspondence were enclosed with a letter to His Grace the Archbishop of St. John's from Mr. Leo E. Emerson, Commissioner for Justice and Defence:

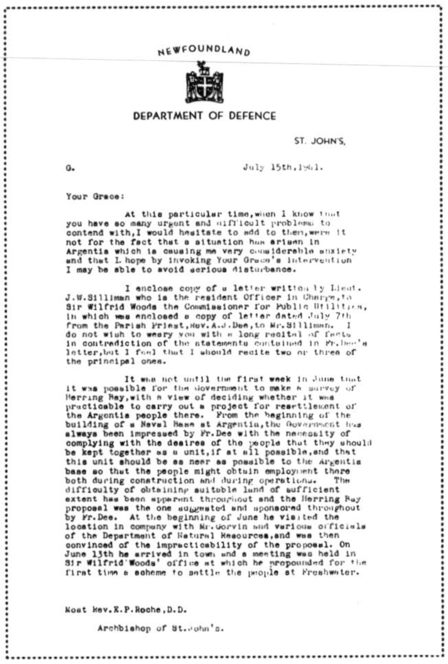

NEWFOUNDLAND

DEPARTMENT OF DEFENCE

ST. JOHN'S,

G. July 15th,1941.

Your Grace:

At this particular time,when I know that you have so many urgent and difficult problems to contend with,I would hesitate to add to them,were it not for the fact that a situation has arisen in Argentia which is causing me very considerable anxiety and that I hope by invoking Your Grace's intervention I may be able to avoid serious disturbance.

I enclose copy of a letter written by Lieut. J.W.Silliman who is the resident Officer in Charge,to Sir Wilfrid Woods the Commissioner for Public Utilities, in which was enclosed a copy of letter dated July 7th from the Parish Priest,Rev.A.J.Dee,to Mr.Silliman. I do not wish to weary you with a long recital of facts in contradiction of the statements contained in Fr.Dee's letter,but I feel that I should recite two or three of the principal ones.

It was not until the first week in June that it was possible for the Government to make a survey of Herring Bay,with a view of deciding whether it was practicable to carry out a project for resettlement of the Argentia people there. From the beginning of the building of a Naval Base at Argentia,the Government has always been impressed by Fr.Dee with the necessity of complying with the desires of the people that they should be kept together as a unit,if at all possible,and that this unit should be as near as possible to the Argentia base so that the people might obtain employment there both during construction and during operations. The difficulty of obtaining suitable land of sufficient extent has been apparent throughout and the Herring Bay proposal was the one suggested and sponsored throughout by Fr.Dee. At the beginning of June he visited the location in company with Mr.Gorvin and various officials of the Department of Natural Resources,and was then convinced of the impracticability of the proposal. On June 13th he arrived in town and a meeting was held in Sir Wilfrid Woods' office at which he propounded for the first time a scheme to settle the people at Freshwater.

Most Rev.E.P.Roche,D.D.
Archbishop of St.John's.

July 15th, 1941.

Most Rev. E.P. Roche, D.D.
Archbishop of St. John's.

Your Grace:

At this particular time, when I know that you have so many urgent and difficult problems to contend with, I would hesitate to add to them, were it not for the fact that a situation has arisen in Argentia which is causing me very considerable anxiety and that I hope by invoking Your Grace's intervention, I may be able to avoid serious disturbance.

I enclose copy of a letter written by Lieut. J. W. Silliman who is the resident Officer in Charge, to Sir Wilfrid Woods, the Commissioner for Public Utilities, in which was enclosed a copy of letter dated July 7th from the Parish Priest, Rev. A. J. Dee, to Mr. Silliman. I do not wish to weary you with a long recital of facts in contradiction of the statements contained in Fr. Dee's letter, but I feel that I should recite two or three of the principal ones.

It was not until the first week in June that it was possible for the Government to make a survey of Herring Bay, with a view of deciding whether it was practicable to carry out a project for resettlement of the Argentia people there. From the beginning of the building of a Naval Base at Argentia, the Government has always been impressed by Fr. Dee with the necessity of complying with the desires of the people, that they should be kept together as a unit if at all possible, and that this unit should be as near as possible to the Argentia base so that the people might obtain employment there both during construction and during operations. The difficulty of obtaining suitable land of sufficient extent has been apparent throughout, and the Herring Bay proposal was the one suggested and sponsored throughout by Fr. Dee. At the beginning of June he visited the location in company with Mr. Gorvin and various officials of the Department of Natural Resources, and was then convinced of the impracticability of the proposal. On June 13th he arrived in town, and a meeting was held in Sir Wilfrid Woods' office at which he propounded for the first time a scheme to settle the people at Freshwater. Those with some familiarity with the area were aware of certain very material difficulties, and it was decided to make no definite move to create a village until the area had been properly examined. At this time all the engineers in the Government employ were busily engaged in different parts of the country, and Sir Wilfrid Woods found considerable difficulty in obtaining an engineer to put in charge of the party which would be necessary to examine and report. This party left town however, on June 25th and have been working there ever since. The statement therefore that the Government has been dilatory in dealing with this matter, is incorrect. The Government, it is true, has refused, quite properly, to embark upon any project of this kind until it has been first examined and found feasible.

It is also incorrect to say that temporary habitation is not available. The Government and the American Naval Authorities have a number of houses available in Placentia, which can be placed at the immediate disposal of those people whose removal is now necessary.

The technical position at the present time is that about nineteen families are under notice, given under the Defence Regulations made under the Emergency Powers Act, to quit their houses by today. They have been awarded compensation and paid in full, and I understand have accepted the awards without demur.

I understand from Mr. H.A. Winter, K.C. who has been acting as Government Counsel throughout, that up to a very few days ago he was under the impression that these people were willing to leave. If his impression on this point is correct, and the people now refuse to move, I feel that they will be doing so because of Fr. Dee's advice. In that event I very much fear that two things will happen. The Americans will insist upon possession because they cannot brook delay, and they may enter upon the property and evict the people, as they are of course entitled to do. This will add very considerably to the sadness of the occasion and is likely to result in the development of riotous conditions. If any disorder should occur, I fail to see how I can exempt Fr. Dee from inclusion in such proceedings as may be taken.

In the hope that the situation may be saved to some extent, I have sent the Chief of Police to Argentia today to interview Fr. Dee and those people now to be moved, and to study the situation on the spot, so that I may have first hand information as to the feelings of the people and of the possible consequences or formal action on the part of the American or Newfoundland Authorities. I expect him to return tomorrow night, when I will have a more detailed knowledge of the situation.

In the meantime, I shall be most grateful if Your Grace would be able to give some thought to what I consider a grave problem, and to consider whether the situation is one in which you may decide to exercise either your power over, or your influence with the Parish Priest. I am at your disposal for a discussion of the situation at any time, and I trust that you will not hesitate to call me into conference if I can further enlighten you on the facts or the situation.

I have the honour to be,
Your Grace's obedient servant,
L. E.. Emerson
Commissioner for Justice and Defence.

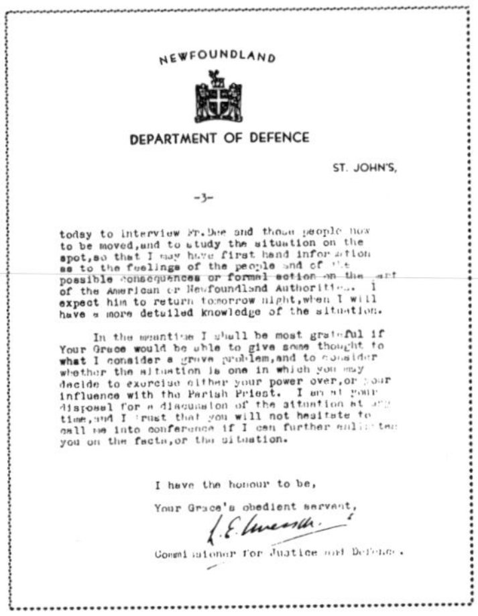
NEWFOUNDLAND

DEPARTMENT OF DEFENCE

ST. JOHN'S,

-3-

today to interview Fr.Dee and those people now to be moved,and to study the situation on the spot,so that I may have first hand information as to the feelings of the people and of the possible consequences or formal action on the part of the American or Newfoundland Authorities. I expect him to return tomorrow night,when I will have a more detailed knowledge of the situation.

In the meantime I shall be most grateful if Your Grace would be able to give some thought to what I consider a grave problem,and to consider whether the situation is one in which you may decide to exercise either your power over,or your influence with the Parish Priest. I am at your disposal for a discussion of the situation at any time,and I trust that you will not hesitate to call me into conference if I can further enlighten you on the facts,or the situation.

I have the honour to be,
Your Grace's obedient servant,
L. E. Emerson
Commissioner for Justice and Defence.

**On July 17 a telegram was sent the Governor, Sir Humphrey Walwyn, and is repeated verbatim:**

COPY OF TELEGRAM

Argentia, July
17th, 1941

To Sir Humphrey Walwyn, K.C.M.G.,
Governor and Chairman Commission of Govt. St. John's.
Your Excellency we the people of Argentia and Marquise would like to advise your Excellency that because of the procrastination of the heads of some departments of Government re our resettlement and because of the mental anguish suffered and in some cases physical suffering endured since last January and because the time is getting short and

very little definite action towards rehabilitation has been taken we are standing on our rights as human beings as well as British subjects stop therefore we have decided not to move from our present homes stop from January till now we willingly cooperated and trusted to the government to help us resettle ourselves and many of us did move from our homes but now we are determined to stay until such time as Government shows its willingness to establish us as a community as near as possible to our traditional homes stop because of this we demand an immediate report of the survey of the area chosen and we demand also that roads be made and land cleared to facilitate placing material for homes on the ground stop we feel this should have been done long before by Government which is responsible for people's well being stop flesh and blood is equally important as war emergency stop we request answer immediately to Chairman Resettlement Committee stop further procrastination might be disastrous stop respectfully subscribed.

| | |
|---|---|
| A. J. Dee, P.P. | John Maher. |
| J. J. Hunt, C.C. | John Healey. |
| P. J. O'Reilly, DD. | Richard Healey. |
| Francis Maher. | Thomas Cooney. |

Freshwater, the site chosen, was a tiny community of seven families, situated about a mile from the base. It had been given its name about 300 years before by English fishermen who landed there to get their supply of drinking water from a brook running to the sea from a large pond some distance away. The French fishermen who also used this brook had named it *La Fontaine.*

When the Argentia people had made certain that the great majority were well pleased with the location, the Resettlement Committee wrote to W. W. Woods:

The Presbytery,
Argentia,
July 17, 1941.

Sir W.W Woods, K.C.M.G.
Commissioner for Public Utilities,
St. John's.
Sir:

Through other correspondence you may have learned that the people of Argentia are completely fed up with the procrastination we have received from your Department. Any promises that we have received from your end have been subject to change, and to our bitter experience have been most changeable. Therefore we demand now, as has been suggested before, that you will exercise your authority as Commissioner for Public Utilities to have every facility of your Department used for the People of Argentia.

Firstly; that a Government Purchasing agent should in conjunction with the Argentia Resettlement Committee procure and purchase lumber for buildings.

Secondly; that roads be made immediately through the area selected.

Thirdly; that machinery suitable for clearing ground be put in operation.

Fourthly; that trucks and drivers belonging to the Highroads Department will be placed at the disposal of the people for the Purpose of cartage to the new Settlement.

Fifthly; that such commodities as cement, nails, felt, fabric board, or any other building material that may be necessary for the building of these houses, be admitted to the Country free of duty.

Sixthly; that a communal sewerage system that will not pollute the American Military and Naval necessities be installed.

In conclusion, we wish to state that we want immediate action in all of the above demands.

Sgd:
Chairman Resettlement
Committee.
Members Resettlement
Committee.

In late August, with no reply received, they began work on the new settlement—a tremendous undertaking, especially when time was of the essence. A survey had to be done and the necessary equipment brought in to make a road through a thickly wooded hill, almost at right angles to the existing road in the valley. Great difficulty was experienced in obtaining labour and machinery for this all-important project. Finally a road was bulldozed and 79 plots cleared, each with a frontage of 80 feet and a rearage of 400 feet. Those who were about to build houses there had to have their materials hauled over this almost impassable road, in order to make their homes at least habitable before winter set in. Some people purchased land in the valley, but not much land was available there at that time.

On August 30 the American Flag was raised in Marquise and the building of the Army Post known as Fort McAndrew began. The residents of that community were then given final notice to evacuate, and by the end of October the last family had departed.

In the meantime the price of building materials had soared, as had the hourly pay demanded by carpenters. Many fathers of families were then faced with a dilemma—whether to quit their newly acquired jobs on the Base and build their homes themselves, or hire a carpenter. Senior citizens had to locate carpenters and purchase material as best they could. There were contractors, but some of them had taken on more than they could achieve in the short time available, and in fact, winter did overtake the construction of some homes.

The request made by the Resettlement Committee to have the duty on building materials lifted, and also a suggestion that the Government pay the Newfoundland Railway the freight charges, were both refused. These concessions would have meant a great deal to the people who had been treated so unfairly. Nor was the request for the provision of a communal sewerage disposal system granted, although now a serious health hazard would be created by people living in such close proximity to one another. (In fact, ten more years passed before the town was incorporated and a water and sewerage system installed.) However, the Newfoundland Government did pay property owners the expenses

The American Flag is raised at Fort McAndrew

Aerial View of Fort McAndrew (Marquise). The large buildings are new ones built by the Americans; they include a hospital and a print shop. The Marquise houses in the photo had been brought up from the meadows on skids by the Americans and arranged in a row. They were completely remodelled inside and rented to American civilians and Newfoundlanders working on the Base; the little community was given the name "Hollywood" by the Americans. The homes were later destroyed. Their former owners included: Joseph Sampson, Bernard Dollmont, Fergus Ryan, Matilda Hunt, Alec Maher, John Maher, Marcellus Maher, Frank Maher, Michael Dunphy and Bill Maher.

incurred while moving from their homes to temporary accommodations and finally to their new homes.

The people then attempted to put their lives together again as best they could, but the peace and tranquillity to which they had been accustomed were gone forever. Living beside a Base in wartime was not conducive to one's peace of mind, especially since a blackout was never enforced in Freshwater. One could not help thinking of the possibility of another Pearl Harbour, and daily reminders of the continual bombings being carried out on the other side of the Atlantic by both sides did nothing to allay our concern. However, thanks to the vigilance which must have prevailed on land, sea and air, no incident ever occurred that would have endangered the lives of the residents of Freshwater.

Because of its adjacency to the Base, the town continued to grow and prosper. A church, presbytery, and school were soon built, and so Holy Rosary Parish was literally transplanted from Argentia to Freshwater. Three new areas of the town were soon developed and populated, mainly by a younger generation and by people from other parts of Newfoundland who had found permanent employment on the Base after the construction boom had ended. The school population grew from 60 pupils in 1942 to just over 500 in the early 1960s.

After the war ended the American servicemen were permitted to bring their families to Argentia, but because there was insufficient housing on the Base at first, many of them rented apartments in Freshwater. This added considerably to the economy of the town.

In 1953 a large modern school was erected at the entrance to Freshwater, with a gymnasium said to be one of the finest in Newfoundland, and a convent was built for the Sisters of the Presentation Order. The small Post Office was replaced by a new Federal building, a town hall which also housed the public library was built, and the people had the security of having their own firefighting equipment as well as dedicated crew of local firefighters.

When two cultures meet one is bound to have some effect on the other to a larger or lesser degree. There may be some doubt as to whether the Americans were changed in any way by our culture, but they had some influence on our lifestyle and customs. However, some of these changes might have come about anyway because of the advent of television into our homes, and also as a result of our becoming a part of Canada in 1949.

Since the American children attended school in Freshwater for a number of years, a change in accent, particularly with our children and young adults, became most noticeable. There were also social changes; children's birthday parties, bridal and baby showers, and Hallowe'en trick-or-treating had been unheard of prior to our exposure to the Americans. Our traditional menu was expanded to include such dishes as pizza, hamburgers, hotdogs, chili and sandwiches. The terms *girlfriend, boyfriend* and *baby-sitter* were added to our vocabulary, along with *penny, nickel* and *dime.*

Most of the residents of Argentia whose homes were expropriated have now passed away. They were heroic people who, in a comparatively short time following their resettlement, had provided comfortable homes once more for their families under very difficult circumstances. May their children, grandchildren, and generations yet to come, know and appreciate the traumatic experience so unexpectedly thrust upon their ancestors.

## Chapter Seven

# COMPENSATION

FOLLOWING THEIR JANUARY 1, 1941 MEETING THE ARGENTIA residents had requested the Commission of Government to set up a Compensation Board immediately to assess the value of each householder's property.

On January 19 Mr. W. W. Woods informed Philip Lewis that the U.S. Government had agreed in principle to the appointment of a Board to deal with these compensation cases. He also stated that the exact position of the U.S. Government in relation to awards made by the Board would be settled at a conference in London, and that the Commission of Government would press for a satisfactory settlement through its representative Commissioners Emerson and Penson.

Following the decision at the conference, the British Government established and guaranteed the final amount of the awards, and also dealt with any questions raised by the U.S. Government concerning this matter. The U.S. Government paid the British, the British paid the Commission of Government, and the Commission of Government made the payments to the people.

Mr. Woods had made it known that those who had already vacated their homes, or had agreed to vacate them, could

(a) settle for full payment of their property by direct negotiation with the Government,
(b) request an interim payment while waiting further negotiation, or
(c) await the setting up of the Compensation Board,

but how could these people place a dollar value on their home and land? It is most likely that the majority chose to appear before the Compensation Board Tribunal. Mr. Justice Higgins had been named chairman in January, but he was powerless to determine the value of property until the Tribunal was appointed.

On March 6 His Excellency the Governor in Commission finally appointed the Tribunal, consisting of Mr. John Boyd Baird and Mr. Francis William Bradshaw with Justice Higgins as chairman. Mr. Harry Winter Q.C. was named Government Counsel while Philip J. Lewis would act on behalf of the people. Mr. Lewis had to ensure that all wills pertaining to the lands in question had

Argentia in early 1941, as seen from the deck of the USS *Richard Peck*

to be probated and letters of administration provided where necessary.

There was a great discrepancy between the awards made to the people of the Argentia Peninsula and those made to the Marquise residents. The latter group may have had more land under cultivation but the homes in both communities were quite similar. In fact there should not have been as much distinction made where the value of houses was concerned, because as the saying goes, "a man's home is his castle." The people on the peninsula received an average of about $3000; since they had to leave their homes at a very difficult time of year, and in many cases had to make a second move, they should have been given special consideration for the disturbance.

When the Board recessed in July, both Judge Higgins and Mr. Winter agreed with Mr. Lewis that the awards were inadequate, and attempted to have them supplemented. Mr. Winter was to take up the matter with the Commission of Government; he would urge them to give a guaranty to protect the people against financial loss, or request permission from them to go to Washington to negotiate the matter with the American Government. It is not known if Mr. Winter was successful in carrying out these intentions, but when sittings resumed the Marquise people were awarded double the amount paid to the Argentia peninsula residents. Should not the latter have had their awards supplemented then? This would have meant a great deal to a householder who had to rebuild a home and who had been dispossessed of a considerable part of his livelihood.

On the whole the people of both the Argentia Peninsula **and** Marquise were inadequately compensated. Although many formal protests were made to the Commission of Government by people who felt they were underpaid, particularly with reference to disturbance rights, the awards were not supplemented. There was no legal recourse, since no question of law was involved.

The final notice, sent to the householders after compensation had been made, read as follows:

"The Defence (requisition of land) Regulations made under the Emergency Powers Defence Act 1940 on the 28th day of December, A.D., 1940.

I have to notify you that the lands and buildings lately belonging to and occupied by you at Argentia, for which said lands and buildings payment has been awarded, are required for occupation by the Government of Newfoundland not later than. . Take notice, therefore, that the said premises must be completely vacated by you and peaceably yielded up to the Government of Newfoundland, its servants, agents, on or before the date mentioned.

Signed: W. W. Woods
Commissioner for Public
Utilities"

Looking back from a distance of 50 years, one has to marvel at the acquiescence of the Argentia people (only three made any effort at refusal to move; two of those had been comparatively well compensated, while the third had no claim to any property). Was it because they were descendants of a long line of fishermen-farmers who were accustomed to the vagaries of the weather, sea and soil, and prepared to expect disaster at any time? Had some other community in Newfoundland been chosen, would the people have co-operated with the authorities in the same way, even allowing for the war emergency? Would they have vacated their homes before adequate compensation had been paid? Would they have demanded that a suitable site be selected and cleared before vacating? Or would resistance have accomplished anything under the prevailing circumstances? The people of Argentia had always been law-abiding citizens and this was certainly proven when they so peacefully gave up their property, leaving behind forever the place they had always known as home.

Over the past 50 years, the question has often been raised as to whom the area would revert to when the 99-year lease to the U.S.A. has expired. Now that the closure of the Base is to take place around 1995, at which time the assets will be turned over to the Canadian Government, the question has taken on a new and greater significance.

The infrastructure of this Naval Facility would be a great asset to the economy of the area if companies could be induced to come to the region, but the five towns in the area would have to amalgamate before an Industrial Park could be set up. Of course the United States would have to carry out an environmental cleanup and also surrender its Right of Return, in spite of the 99-year lease.

The Argentia Area Development Association and the Argentia Area Chamber of Commerce are endeavouring to see that these assets at our doorstep will be utilized in such a way as to boost the economy of the region. Many areas throughout the world have experienced a temporary crisis when military bases have closed, but because of the utilization of the assets to attract business, their economy has even taken an upturn. With foresight and proper planning this can also be achieved in Argentia.

---

NOTE: *The names of the dispossessed householders, and the amounts of compensation they received, can be found in Appendices I and II at the back of this book. The figures were obtained from the Provincial Archives.*

# Chapter Eight

# THE BASE

THE ANGLO-AMERICAN AGREEMENT FOR A 99-YEAR LEASE, enacted on June 11, 1941, was known officially as the American Bases Act. When the lease took effect on June 14 construction had already begun, because of the emergency that existed. The greatest haste was necessary to build this all-important defence post.

## CONSTRUCTION

Newfoundland men and women came by the thousands from all parts of the island, and there were jobs for all according to their ability and their choice. It was estimated that at the height of construction ten thousand people were directly or indirectly employed.

The outbreak of the war was deplored by everyone (although not many shared the sentiments of the fellow who, staggering home from his favourite pub, was overheard muttering "God bless Hitler"). Nevertheless, the employment made available was a benefit. Newfoundlanders had just experienced ten years of economic depression, during which many people had to try to exist on six cents a day, so the prosperity the war brought to the island was most welcome.

People left the fishery, the lumber woods and the mines to take advantage of the employment opportunities at Argentia, even

USS *Richard Peck*

though sufficient living accommodations had not yet been provided. A large ship, the *U.S.S. Richard Peck*, was brought in from the U.S. to provide quarters for a limited number of servicemen and civilians. The fishermen brought their boats and moored them in the harbour; other workers lived in tents adjacent to the Base, while some lodged with relatives or friends.

The question of wages for Newfoundland workers now became a cause for concern. A member of the Argentia committee contacted Mr. Lewis in early January, informing him that work was beginning there and that a Mr. Hall was hiring men. They were not satisfied with the offer of 25 cents per hour for labourers and 40 cents per hour for carpenters, and he asked Mr. Lewis' advice on the matter. As Mr. Lewis wrote to Father Dee on January 7, 1941:

In the foreground is Traverse's Cove. Across the water the USS *Richard Peck* is moored at the North Side of the Base. The fishing boats in the picture belong to the Argentia people.

> I told him to interview Hall and to protest the payment of this rate, but not to refuse to accept it. I suggested that the men go to work at this rate of pay, but reserving all rights to have the question of wages reviewed at the proper time by the proper authorities.

The *Evening Telegram* reported on the matter:

> A meeting was held at Argentia under the chairmanship of Rev. Fr. Dee at which the Government was represented by Sir Wilfrid Woods, Commissioner for Public Utilities; Sir John Puddester, Commissioner for Public Health; and Honourable J. H. Gorvin, Commissioner for Natural Resources. On the question of wages to be paid for unskilled labour, this matter was also brought before the meeting by the executive of the citizen's committee. The people were under the impression that the Government had interfered and fixed the rate at 25 cents. (It was reported that the

Commission of Government had requested this rate of pay, fearing a higher wage would entice many Government employees to leave their present positions and seek employment on the Base). The Commissioners assured them this was not so. It was also rumoured that the Water Street merchants who had quite an influence over the Government, had requested a low wage for the Newfoundland workers, fearing an exodus of their employees. Mr. Lewis put the people's case in the matter to the commissioners, emphasizing that as far as wages at Argentia were concerned, the people wanted the right to deal directly with the American authorities without Government interference.

Although the Government denied interference, the wage imbalances continued for many years.

It is impossible to give a detailed description of the actual construction of this important Base, especially when such great urgency was necessary. In spite of a typical Newfoundland winter the work continued 24 hours a day, with floodlights used at night until a blackout became necessary. Warehouses, office buildings, docking facilities, and temporary barracks for the workmen all had to be constructed with speed, while acres of peat bog, sometimes more than 20 feet deep, had to be removed and dumped into the sea. In the beginning the majority of the workmen were Newfoundlanders; they soon became quite adept at operating and repairing the many kinds of machinery used, and in many other trades as well. Mr. Davis, Project Manager for the contractors, paid them high tribute, and it is chiefly to their credit that this great Base was completed in such a short period of time. There was also a considerable variety of work for girls and women, and at the peak of construction almost 200 were employed. They worked in the laundry, the mess halls, the ship's stores and as telephone operators, stenographers and secretaries.

## THE ATLANTIC CHARTER

In July 1941 President Roosevelt suggested to Prime Minister Churchill that they meet in some secluded and remote area. They decided on Placentia Bay. The following excerpt from H. V. Morton's book "The Atlantic Meeting" describes the preparations:

> Britain's latest battleship, the *Prince of Wales* and an escort of destroyers were placed under orders; a special train had to be chartered to take the Prime Minister, the chiefs of staff and their advisors to the port of embarkation; special food and other stores had to be ordered. Clerks, secretaries and a staff of cipher clerks had to be sent ahead. It was essential that none of these people should have the slightest idea of what was happening or where he was going. Obviously the utmost secrecy was necessary because of the numerous German submarines in the north Atlantic at that time.

It was also essential that President Roosevelt's whereabouts be kept secret. He was thought to have boarded his yacht, apparently to take a holiday cruise, but at some distance off he and his staff transferred to the *U.S.S. Augusta* and set course for Placentia Bay.

The *Prince of Wales* arrived off Argentia on Saturday morning of the 9th of August. The *Augusta* had already arrived, and it must have been a magnificent spectacle as these two great ships, surrounded by cruisers, destroyers, corvettes, and minesweepers, lay at anchor near Ship Harbour off Argentia.

On Saturday afternoon the American sailors presented each British sailor with a carton containing an orange, two apples, 200 cigarettes and a half pound of cheese. These items would indeed be considered a grand treat by the English sailors because of the serious food shortage in England at that time. On Sunday a joint church service was held aboard the *Prince of Wales*, in which Churchill and Roosevelt took part along with British and American Officers, sailors and marines.

Maintaining strict secrecy during the three-day stay of these world leaders was in itself a major feat. There was a total blackout at Argentia, no telephone communication was permitted, no person was allowed to enter or leave the Base, and even the train was held up outside the terminus.

This was the setting for the drawing up of the famed *Atlantic Charter*—a joint declaration by the President of the United States of America and the Prime Minister of Great Britain. It was a pledge of their united faith in freedom and their hopes for a better world for the future. This document eventually became the foundation of our United Nations Charter. Not until after the end of hostilities was it disclosed where the famous conference had taken place.

Roosevelt and Churchill meet off Argentia

*NOTE: The 50th anniversary of this momentous event—the first meeting of Churchill and Roosevelt and the drawing up of the most remarkable document in history—was commemorated on Sunday August 11, 1991, at both Ship Harbour and Argentia. Mr. Churchill's daughter Lady Mary Soames and Mr. Roosevelt's granddaughter Ms. Laura Roosevelt, as well as many other distinguished dignitaries, were present for the event. On Sunday morning the two ladies visited the monument in Ship Harbour which had been erected in 1976 to commemorate the drawing up of the Charter. Afterwards they expressed their appreciation of the welcome they had received and their great pleasure at having had the opportunity to visit the community so near the site where history had been made. Church services, similar to the one held on board the Prince of Wales at the time of the conference, took place at both Ship Harbour and Argentia.*

## OPERATIONS

The importance of the Base at Argentia soon became evident. It was from there that the anti-submarine patrols flew over the North Atlantic and were instrumental in subduing the German submarine menace. One of those patrols captured a German weather station set up on the coast of Greenland, before it was able to transmit any weather reports.

It was a pilot on patrol from Argentia who sent out the famous message "Sighted sub, sank same." That submarine was said to be off Red Island. In fact, German submarines were attacked and sunk at the very entrance to Argentia harbour. Argentia also served as a base for supplying, servicing and repairing the ships of the Allies.

The United States was now provoked into entering the war. On Sunday morning, December 7, 1941, 350 Japanese bombers attacked the Hawaiian Island Base of Pearl Harbour where a great fleet of American ships lay at anchor and numerous aircraft were assembled on the surrounding airfields. Within two hours the Base was reduced to a scene of death and destruction, leaving the Japanese in total control of the Pacific. On the following day President Roosevelt asked Congress to declare a state of war between the U.S. and Japan. Thirty-three minutes later came the formal declaration, and the U.S. joined the world conflict.

Following this turn of events, hundreds of ships relied on the Base in Argentia for their needs—British, Norwegian, Danish, Panamanian, French, Dutch, Canadian, Russian, as well as U.S. Coast Guard cutters, seaplane tenders, transports, battleships, cargo ships, cruisers, destroyers, patrol crafts, escorts, frigates, and corvettes. In the spring of 1945, two thousand tonnes of provisions were issued, vast amounts of diesel oil were supplied, and the cafeteria and ships' stores were hard pressed to meet all the demands.

A fleet of small vessels, known as the Atlantic Weather Patrol, was also based at Argentia. These boats, which monitored points all over the North Atlantic, were equipped to report weather conditions and predictions, thus contributing to the safety of troops and supply ships crossing the Atlantic. Another important unit was the Ice Patrol, which was carried on by sea and air; this patrol reported on the positions of icebergs and predicted their routes—again an important factor in the safety of Allied shipping in the North Atlantic.

During the war years many German prisoners of war, survivors of U-boats hit by U.S. bombers, were interned at Argentia. Two captive German destroyers and two captive submarines manned by American crews also put in at Argentia for repairs, fuel and supplies on the way back to the United States.

With all the activity on both land and sea there were bound to be casualties. Consequently a site was chosen for a cemetery on what was known to the people of Argentia as *Long Hill*, but renamed *Boot Hill* by the Americans. The bodies buried there were exhumed after the war and brought back to the United States.

American Cemetery on Boot Hill (Long Hill)

## TREASON

Judging from the number of graves on Boot Hill there must have been many attempts at sabotage and espionage. Traitors were executed by firing squad and buried at Boot Hill, on the opposite side from people who were killed by accident. Their graves were unmarked, and their bodies were also exhumed after the war. It is told that an American civilian who had built a house near the entrance to Freshwater was found to have a wireless set inside the casing of the chimney. No doubt this was used to report to the enemy any useful information, especially the departure of shipping.

Memorial Day Service, 1942

Brother Francis Foran, a native son of Argentia, has related an incident in his unpublished memoirs. On one occasion while his mother was the lightkeeper at Point Latine, an officer knocked at the door of the lighthouse and informed her that if she heard rifle shots she need not be alarmed. Behind him she saw two servicemen carrying rifles, and with them a third person. It was rumoured afterwards that this third person had deserted his post on shoreline patrol and was then being shot by firing squad. Because it was wartime, desertion was considered a grave offence, especially since German submarines were known to be lurking in the immediate area.

### THE U.S.S. *PRAIRIE*

The fire on board the huge supply ship *U.S.S. Prairie* was rumoured to have been caused by enemy action, although no hint of this was ever given by the U.S. Navy. According to an article in *LIFE Magazine* the Navy announced that on May 27 the *Prairie* caught fire while docked at ________,* burned for nearly five hours and was finally saved from destruction with the loss of only two lives.

The article went on to say that the accidental conflagration started on another ship tied astern to the *Prairie,* but flames whipped up by a 40-knot gale rapidly spread to the destroyer tender. Immediately other boats helped the burning supply ship snap her chains and hawsers and move away from the dock. Crews from nearby craft joined the perilous firefighting on the

* The location was not given in *LIFE Magazine,* probably because security requirements did not permit it.

Artist's Conception of the Mother Ship U.S.S. *Prairie* (left) and Destroyers. This is a reproduction of a colour painting which appeared in *LIFE* Magazine on May 25, two days before the fire. (Note: The proportion of the *Prairie* to the large destroyers gives an idea of its immense size.)

smoking, exploding inferno. Aboard the tender were 600 tons of high explosives, 300 depth charges, 103 warheads for torpedoes, 12,000 gallons of diesel oil and 1,000,000 gallons of fuel oil. Although the fire raged along the entire starboard side and internally at eleven other points, the leaping flames were finally halted just one compartment away from the munition stores.

In the fight to prevent an explosion two sailors were killed and two seriously wounded. The damage to the ship was so extensive that she had to go back to the U.S. for repairs, following which she returned to Argentia.

On the day of the accident I was teaching school in Freshwater. At about 11 a.m. Miss Clara Hunt, the teacher from the other classroom, came to my door. She informed me that Father Dee had just brought his aunt, who was residing with him in Argentia, to stay with a friend in Freshwater, because there was a fire on board the *Prairie* and an explosion was feared.

This was startling news. I could not dismiss my pupils without giving them a reason, nor could I tell them what might happen. The anxiety of that next endless hour remains vividly in my memory. But lunch time finally arrived and I breathed a great sigh of relief as they all left for home. I was not thinking so much of myself should an explosion occur, but of the reaction of the 30 young children under my care.

I didn't realize the danger we had been in until later. An account of the incident in one of our local newspapers soon afterwards stated that the explosion would have been felt at a

Fire Aboard the *Prairie*

distance of 70 miles. I shudder to think of what would have happened to us here in Freshwater, just a mile or so from the Base.

The foregoing is just a brief sketch of the activity that took place at this most important defence post. A high ranking British Officer is said to have remarked, and I quote: "Without Argentia I doubt if we could have gotten over the hump that meant the winning of the war."

# Chapter 9

# REMOVAL OF CEMETERIES

UNLIKE THOSE NEWFOUNDLANDERS WHO HAD TO LEAVE THEIR homes during the large Resettlement Program of 1954-1972, the Argentia people were at least able to have their departed ones moved to the new location. The American authorities had proposed that the three cemeteries in Argentia be cemented over, but Father Dee would not agree to this plan. It was then decided that the three be relocated as one whenever a suitable site could be found in Freshwater, and that the work of exhumation and re-interment would be undertaken by the U.S. Government.

Again they experienced the same frustrations as those that had accompanied the preparation of the town site. After some delays a piece of land was purchased through a private sale, and a survey was made. Now a road had to be constructed to connect the new cemetery with the existing road in the settlement, and an extensive excavation made for reception of the remains.

On October 1, 1941 Mr. Emerson, the Commissioner for Justice, granted a licence to Dr. Alexander Bishop, Chief Health Inspector of the Department of Public Health and Welfare, for the removal of the bodies. Below is a copy of that license.

### TO WHOM IT MAY CONCERN

In pursuance of the provisions of the Act 21 George V, Chapter 12, entitled "An Act to Provide for the Exhumation or Removal of Dead Bodies", licence is hereby granted to Dr. Alexander Bishop, Chief Health Inspector of the Department of Public Health and Welfare, to remove to some other cemetery or suitable burying grounds the bodies or remains of all persons buried in the three Roman Catholic cemeteries at Argentia.

The exhumation and removal of all such bodies or remains shall be carried out under the supervision of said Chief Health Inspector subject to such precautions, if any, as may be prescribed by the Department of Public Health and Welfare.

Dated at St. John's this 1st day of October, A.D. 1941.
Commissioner for Justice.

A formal request was made on October 5 to the Department of Public Works that the road to the cemetery be constructed and the excavation made. On October 15 Father Dee received a letter from Mr. Manning, the Secretary for Public Works, stating that because of a shortage of labourers and dump trucks they would not be in a position to build the cemetery road; the shortage was due to the work being done on the new settlement road. Public Works had written the American authorities requesting them to undertake the necessary construction work. The Americans had agreed, but thought it advisable to defer the work until spring.

And so in the spring of 1942 the vault was excavated and the gruesome task of exhuming the bodies was begun. The remains of each individual were enclosed in a separate box for removal, and the funerals to the new cemetery took place at night, to minimize the traumatic effect on the relatives of the dead. The common vault was in the shape of a cross, with the coffins placed in tiers of three and the headstones and markers placed around the sides. Individuals who had had family members pass away just prior to the American takeover were permitted to exhume the bodies themselves and bury them in a plot of their own choice at the new cemetery.

In the meantime it was determined that more land was needed, and on July 7 Father Dee applied to the Department of Natural Resources for a Crown grant of 3 1/4 acres in order to extend the plot already purchased. Considerable delay was caused by arguments about the amount of land required; three Government Departments became involved. The Americans were most anxious to have the matter completed since it was holding up their construction.

The work was finally completed in August. The following report on the procedure was obtained from the Provincial Archives:

> To the Honourable Commissioner for Public Health and Welfare
>
> Report of the Chief Health Inspector on the Exhumation and removal of the dead bodies from the Cemeteries at Argentia.
>
> Acting upon your instructions and invested with the necessary legal authority from the Justice Department, I have just completed the excavation, removal and re-burying of six hundred and twenty-five bodies or remains, from the three Roman Catholic Cemeteries at Argentia; the actual work having been conducted between July 14th and August 10th, which time included transportation to and from Argentia.
>
> Previous to July 14th two other visits were made to Argentia to make arrangements for the actual starting of the work.
>
> Not having had the slightest experience in such a big undertaking, and being unable to obtain any worthwhile information locally, it was with a great sense of fear that I undertook to supervise a project for which I had developed an increasing dread ever since I was first chosen to do the work in September past, not so much because of the gruesome nature of the work, as to the sentimentality of the people.
>
> There were three Cemeteries at Argentia, the oldest one having headstones dating back as far as 1772, and the new one

having been started about 1924—the intermediate one having been started some time in the middle of the nineteenth century. In each of the three Cemeteries there had been recent burials, so that it could be said that all three were in use up to about eighteen months or two years ago. It was found that no records were kept, either of the dates of burials, or of the location of the graves, and we had to rely in most instances on our own ability to find the graves. Some were marked with headstones, but in many cases we found that they were further from the graves than would ordinarily be expected.

Previous to starting the exhumation a plan was made of each Cemetery, and any information such as that found on head stones was recorded and some photographs were taken. All this information is in the hands of the Naval authorities. The headstones and other markers were then removed, and our own markers placed instead, upon which we had placed any information required by us. While this was being done, we had made up at the mill a number of boxes in two standard sizes, 12 x 12 x 27 inches, and 12 x 12 x 84 inches. The larger cases were for the reception of bodies in coffins that we were able to move intact, and the others for the reception of remains. These boxes were made of three- quarter inch plywood, and were ordered from the mill in quantities as the work progressed.

The actual work of exhumation started early on the afternoon of July 17th at which time our help consisted of an American Foreman, a shovel operator and a timekeeper with about ten Newfoundland workmen. The Newfoundlanders, who had been for the past two days working with us removing the headstones and replacing our own markers, decided that in consideration of the danger to which they might expose themselves, it would be reasonable for them to expect more pay at this particular job than they received at their regular work, whereupon they made their demands to the Superintendent, who for some reason (which I did not feel was my business) did not see fit to give them an increase, with the result that the men gave up their job at the Base altogether and returned to their homes.

To find a new staff of workmen, volunteers were called for from American workmen, when eight new members were added to the three which I had already had, making a total of twelve including the man Morcombe who I had with me from St. John's. After tea that day we worked with our new staff or crew, and by dark that night we were getting to be fairly proficient in the work. We continued to work each day, including Sundays, from daylight to dark, finishing one cemetery at a time, and transferring our equipment to another place.

After our first day's work it was found that for many reasons we would have to more or less live on the job. Two shacks were provided for us, one as a mortuary room, and the other as living quarters, where we could wash, change our clothing and eat our meals. These two shacks were moved with us as we transferred our activities from one Cemetery to another.

The actual digging was done by a combination of mechanical shovelling and hand labour. With the mechanical shovel, a long trench 6 or 7 feet deep was made on the outside of the Cemetery along by the side of the coffins; then by scraping off the side of the bank we were able to reach the sides of the coffins, after which the mechanical shovel stopped and hand labour was used to finish removing the clay and lifting out the coffin, or the remains, and placing them in the specially prepared boxes, taking note of even the slightest means of identification and recording it on the covers of the boxes. Depending on the state in which we found the bodies on any given day, we would either bury them at once or keep them in our mortuary shed to await a sufficient number to make a worthwhile load for a large truck.

Burying: In the new Cemetery at Freshwater, a large T-shape grave was dug, with the stem of the T pointing east, and the top running North and South. The longest part was from North to South and measured over two hundred feet by fifteen feet and the stem of the T measured about eighty feet by twenty feet.

In the longest part of the T, along its West side, a line of large boxes was placed side by side (feet to the East) and at the foot of these were placed small boxes, end to end, and three feet away from the large boxes, thus giving two lines of boxes along nearly the whole length from South to North. In this long trench we placed the bodies or remains of all the persons who we were able to identify or about whom we had sufficient information that may be useful at a later date for someone else to identify them by, such as the body of a young or old male or female person taken from a grave next to a certain family plot. Requests were made by some of the residents to have some bodies placed side by side, although, in the old Cemeteries they were separated, and also, some requests to have separated in the new graves bodies that lay side by side in the old Cemeteries, both of which was done when it was at all possible. We were most careful at all times to keep families together when placing them in the new grave. In the case of bodies or remains of which we could find no marks of identification, they were buried in the stem of the T, side by side, and when possible were laid East and West.

When the boxes were first placed in the graves, they were covered with tarpaulins so that if necessary, we could move one or two to replace them with others in order to keep families or friends together. When we were satisfied that we had placed them as well as we could, we had the Surveyors come and take measurements and other details of the position of the boxes, and make a record of names and other identification marks which they are using in the plan which is now being made of the grave, so that, when finished it will be possible to measure from a given point and find any coffin. When this information was collected, there was a plank covering put over the top of the coffins, and the grave was refilled by pushing earth over it with a bulldozer. This practice continued until the whole grave was filled with bodies, covered and graded, so that at least five feet of earth covered each box. Just as I had finished the second Cemetery and was about to move to the third or newest Cemetery (Mount Rosary), I had a delegation come to see me claiming that they were the Managing Committee of the New Cemetery at Freshwater, and informing me that, certain persons were desirous of starting family plots in the new Cemetery and wished me to give them permission to dig graves for the reception of their own relatives. As my license called for the re-burying in some suitable burying ground, I could not but accede to their request, and informed them if they would dig graves of sufficient size and depth, that I would bury the bodies in them. These are known locally as private graves —

Number of bodies and remains disinterred and reinterred 625

175 bodies or remains were placed in 152 boxes, large and small sometimes more than one of a family in one big box. These were all identified.

15 bodies and remains were placed in eleven boxes and were buried in ten private graves.

103 bodies were placed singly in boxes. These bodies or remains could not be identified.

332 remains were placed in thirty-nine small boxes. These could not be identified and were from bodies buried for quite a long time. Sometimes only a few bones remained.

During the whole project (project 500 as it was known by the Contractors) every assistance was given me by the Naval authorities and the Contractors, and we had many visitors of high ranking positions in the Navy and Army as well as several visits from the priests of the parish and outside, as well as some doctors and chaplains from the forces. I was pleased too, to have a visit from Dr. Mosdell, Secretary for the Department of Public Health and Welfare, and to have him see the work actually being done.

Respectfully submitted
A. Bishop
Chief Health Inspector.

Dated at St. John's
August 12th, 1942.

Exhumation of the Graves at Argentia

After this most difficult task was completed, Father Dee expressed to Base Commander Martin his deep appreciation, and the thanks of the people of Freshwater, for the excellent work done, not only in removing the bodies in a satisfactory and respectful manner, but also for the fencing, grading and seeding of the new burial site.

Several efforts were made in recent years to have the Freshwater cemetery declared a national historic site, but without success; it was not considered to be of national interest. Perhaps in the future another appeal may meet with a more sympathetic hearing. The people of Argentia deserve this, since not only were they themselves disturbed, but their departed relatives and friends as well.

The New Cemetery at Freshwater, 1943

Mother in her Garden

## Chapter 10

# FAMILY EXPERIENCES

NO AMOUNT OF MONEY COULD EVER COMPENSATE FOR THE mental and physical suffering caused by the uprooting of people, the destruction of their property, and the disappearance of their way of life. It was a heartrending experience for almost every family.

These are the stories of a cross section of the people of Argentia who had to leave their homes, taking with them only their household belongings, to start life anew. The event, an important one in the annals of Newfoundland's history, was a sad chapter in the lives of these people, many of whom have since passed away, leaving their personal experiences for the most part unrecorded.

### Our Own Experience
**(the Hunt family)**

My Father died in 1924 at the age of 43 and left my mother a widow with seven children ranging in age from 14 years to 7 months. Because my father had a small life insurance policy, Mother did not receive any government help, but had to depend on the produce of our small farm. She grew potatoes, cabbage, carrots, turnip, parsnip, onions, beet and even pumpkins; she kept sheep, poultry, two cows, and a horse to help her with the heavy work. She also cultivated four hayfields to feed the livestock. So, although her family was raised, who can imagine her feelings when presented with the following notice?

Department of Public Works
St.John's, Newfoundland
19th April, 1941.

Sir,

I enclose herewith a copy of an order which I have made under the Defence (Requisitioning of Land) Regulations with respect to an area of land in the vicinity of Argentia.

I am informed that you are the owner of the land which is situated within this area.

I regret to inform you that it will be shortly become necessary to take possession of this property. It is necessary to take possession immediately of all of the land within the area upon which there are no buildings erected and the Order which has been made authorizes this to be done. It is not intended to take possession of any buildings immediately and this is not authorized by the Order. It will shortly be necessary to acquire buildings, but again you will be notified again before this is done.

Under the Order which has been made agents and contractors of the United States Government may go upon your land immediately to start construction work. I hope the entry on your land by the United States Authorities will not cause you serious inconveniences at the present time. It is absolutely necessary as a war measure.

I should be glad to receive from you a claim for damages which will be caused to you by the expropriation of your property. Such a claim can be dealt with by direct agreement or, in due course, by the compensation board set up to deal with such claims.

Yours faithfully,
Commissioner for Public Utilities.

Mrs Mary Hunt,
Argentia.

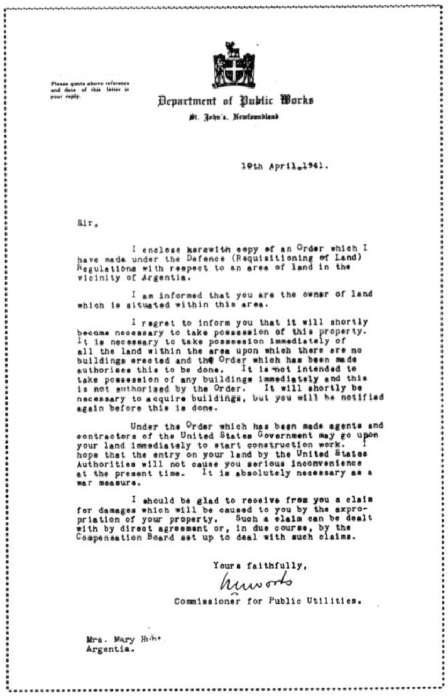

Please quote above reference and date of this letter in your reply.

Department of Public Works
St. John's, Newfoundland

10th April, 1941.

Sir,

I enclose herewith copy of an Order which I have made under the Defence (Requisitioning of Land) Regulations with respect to an area of land in the vicinity of Argentia.

I am informed that you are the owner of land which is situated within this area.

I regret to inform you that it will shortly become necessary to take possession of this property. It is necessary to take possession immediately of all the land within the area upon which there are no buildings erected and the Order which has been made authorises this to be done. It is not intended to take possession of any buildings immediately and this is not authorised by the Order. It will shortly be necessary to acquire buildings, but you will be notified again before this is done.

Under the Order which has been made agents and contractors of the United States Government may go upon your land immediately to start construction work. I hope that the entry on your land by the United States Authorities will not cause you serious inconvenience at the present time. It is absolutely necessary as a war measure.

I should be glad to receive from you a claim for damages which will be caused to you by the expropriation of your property. Such a claim can be dealt with by direct agreement or, in due course, by the Compensation Board set up to deal with such claims.

Yours faithfully,

Commissioner for Public Utilities.

Mrs. Mary Hunt
Argentia.

She then had to dispose of her livestock, and I can vividly remember to see her crying on the day the horse was sold. He had been her greatest help during all the years of struggling to feed her family.

She received the first notice of eviction in August and immediately engaged a contractor to build our new home in Freshwater, giving him the plan and dimensions. She was assured it would be completed in October, but when the time came for us to move out, the house had not even been started. She then had to hire a local carpenter to build a shed on our lot in which to store our furniture and belongings, thus adding to the cost of our new home.

Our House in Marquise

While we were still in Marquise the electric power was cut off, our drinking water polluted, and a deep trench dug in front of the house so that we had to walk on a plank to reach the road. All of the neighbours had left and the local shops closed, leaving us no choice but to seek shelter elsewhere. Since Mother and I were the only members of the family at home by now, her aunt-in-law from Ferndale offered to take us in until our house was ready for occupancy, which we were sure would be before Christmas. Mother then wired my brother Frank, who had joined the Canadian Navy, that he was desperately needed at home to help us pack; luckily he was granted leave.

The Americans had agreed to move the household effects of all of the families, but we were not allowed to take doors or windows even though the houses would be bulldozed soon after being vacated. Since my father had made all of the doors in our house, Mother was determined to take some of them, so she wrapped them in blankets and managed to get them into the truck unnoticed. It was a dull, gloomy October evening and dark was closing in when the last truck with our worldly goods was ready to leave. Then the three of us, with heavy hearts, climbed on board, taking a long last look at our home, knowing that in a matter of days the bulldozers would reduce it to rubble. This was, I know, a heartrending moment for my mother; so it must have been for all of the fathers and mothers of Argentia who were forced to leave their homes and seek temporary living quarters elsewhere.

This was my first visit to the site of our new house, and I wondered as the truck climbed the steep hill, with its wheels sinking in the mud, if the approach would be improved when we finally came to live there. But sad to say, the improvement did not take place for a long, long time.

When the last of our belongings had been stored in the shed we returned in the truck to the bottom of the hill and hired a taxi to take us to Ferndale. When we reached the Devil's Bit—a section of road that got its name because it was extremely steep—it was so bad that the driver could not take us any further. By then it was night and there we were by the side of the road, forlorn and homeless, clutching our few personal belongings. Frank, who had the most cheerful disposition, began to laugh, saying we were now like the Polish refugees.* For some reason this seemed to cheer us up temporarily, and on foot we climbed the Devil's Bit and on into Ferndale. The next day Frank left us to join his ship in Halifax, which further dampened our spirits.

Mother with Family, circa 1928. L. To R. Bride, Mother, Eileen, Michael, Frank, Patricia and Jane. Missing from Photo: Edmund.

As mentioned earlier, we had expected to have our house completed by Christmas at the latest. About once a week Mother would walk from Ferndale to our plot of ground in Freshwater, a distance of about four kilometres. But no start was being made and she could never locate the contractor, who had taken on the building of other houses.

Christmas came and went and it was not till January, four months after we had left Marquise, that on one of her trips she discovered a foundation had been laid. It was, however, very much larger than the one she had specified to the contractor. She was now faced with a dilemma. To have the foundation changed would delay the completion of the building, and to have it left as it was would mean that the house would cost much more. She decided on the latter, even though she did not need a larger house now.

* Hitler had just invaded Poland and many of its citizens were fleeing their country

By March the kitchen was completed, so Mother and I moved into our "one-room apartment" while the carpenters worked on the rest of the house. But soon afterwards they had some dispute with the contractor over wages, and went on strike. She then had to find other carpenters to complete the work, and this proved to be a difficult task since everyone was employed. She eventually got the work done, however, and at last we moved our furniture in from the shed.

Our story did not end there. Mother, who was a patient and tolerant woman, would have accepted all the delays and mishandling; but a couple of the neighbours who also had grievances asked her to join them in taking the contractor to court. To appear in a court of law was the last thing in the world Mother would want, but rather than appear disagreeable she agreed to do so. Of course, nothing was ever gained by it.

In a few short years the family had all married and gone their separate ways, leaving Mother alone in the big house. Like most of the people her age who had been displaced, she never felt at home in Freshwater. Above all she missed her gardens; she attempted to grow a few vegetables but the soil was gritty and her efforts were in vain.

✣ ✣ ✣

*Ms. Ann McGrath has given a very moving account of her departure from her home in Argentia:*

It was a beautiful quiet autumn day that September 1940 when I heard and saw several planes overhead. This was unusual, as the only plane I had ever seen was the German Blimp which had flown over in 1939. How was I to know that this was an aerial survey for a Naval base to be built in Argentia?

Rumours began to fly. "The Americans are going to build a base here." Rumours are usually exaggerated! Not this time! In my wildest imagination I could never envision the course of events that would enfold in the next year—and all the years since then. How could I know that the heart of this sleepy place we call Argentia would be wrenched out to make way for machines of war, and that Sir Winston Churchill's "I have nothing to offer you but blood, sweat and tears" applied to me and to all of the people of Argentia?

In these carefree days of warm and close friendship, the idea of separation was far from my mind—a few planes overhead was exciting and a great conversation piece, but the war was "over there." That September of 1940, holidays over, I returned to school in an effort to complete Grade XI.

That same month the first sea planes arrived, and an old lady remarked, "They are going to build here alright, there's a plane out there with a load of lumber on her deck." The next day the battleship *St. Louis* arrived. Some people, said to be under the command of a retired Admiral, began the process of triangulation. I did not understand what they were talking about, but they hired our motor boat, and my brother to transport them, which was great.

They also hired three or four local men to help. They set the targets on Isaac's Head, John Hunt's Pinnacle, Fox Island and Martin's Hill, all familiar landmarks to me. My father had often taken us in the motor boat to Isaac's and the Pinnacle to gather firewood, pick berries or just play while he cut firewood. When Father Dee came to our home to collect dues he said that everyone would be employed, and we would soon be able to drive to Port-aux-Basques in a bus. In those days the only way to Port-aux-Basques was by train.

In October the SS *Bowditch* arrived. The excitement was building. Father Dee invited the Captain and the crew to the local hall to take part in some entertainment. The Captain reciprocated by inviting the people to what they called a Smoker in the same hall. They had five boxing matches and one wrestling match. They gave out ice cream, cigarettes, etc. all free of charge. I thought it was called a Smoker because they gave out cigarettes. The hall was upstairs over the school. I remember walking up the stairs that November 17, 1940, and seeing rows of black shiny shoes, of sailors all around the boxing ring. They were the best-behaved sailors I have seen since then, and must have been specially trained.

Events were happening fast! A warehouse and an administration building was constructed in Sandy Cove. Sandy Cove was the Terminus for the train and coastal boats and the business centre—the downtown—of Argentia. Bunk houses began to be constructed on Dunphy's Road, very close to where I lived. All of the men were being hired, which was truly a Godsend in these days of the Depression. I believe many people were under the impression that building a Base here meant plenty of work, and all of us living happily employed.

The rumours were on the increase. It was even suggested that people may have to move. That was more than a small mind like mine could absorb—that was surely not true—but it was. Soon we heard that the school would close at Christmas and there would be no C.H.E. exams the following year in Argentia. I decided to sign on in a Fox Harbour school which was half an hour by boat from where I lived. After Christmas I decided to study on my own. Who needs teachers?

Everything was moving very quickly now. Twenty-four families were ordered to evacuate within two weeks or one month. My Father and our neighbours had an interview on December 28, 1940. Following that on January 1, 1941, a meeting of all of the people of Argentia was held. A committee was formed and drew up a set of resolutions to be presented to the Archbishop and the Minister of Defence. I suppose the rest has been recorded in history. For myself, I recall the torment and the anguish of my father, then sixty-eight years old—the meetings, the letters, etc,. Where would we go? What would we do? There were promises of remuneration, but nothing forthcoming.

The contractors built a road down as far as our house; this greatly facilitated our transportation to the church, which was still open, and to Sandy Cove about two miles distant. The bus driver waited for us to come out single file when we spotted the bus, and we knew we could have a free ride. Indeed, it was the bus driver who informed me that "Sir Winston Churchill and President Roosevelt are meeting out there in a ship" which was moored straight out from our house. Little did I realize what history was being made on that day.

The friendly and generous Americans were now becoming part of the lives of the people of Argentia, especially the younger generation. There was a team who began to survey the land all around our houses. They invited themselves in for tea in the afternoon, and one day as one of them related how a bulldozer was lost in the bog, my father said he hoped it would go down five hundred feet to Hell. One of them asked "Is that were Hell is?" That may have been the end of the tea meetings. I cannot recall. I was studying Trigonometry on my own as I related above, and one of the team showed me how to make measurements using my knowledge of Trigonometry. My father was not much in favour of that kind of closeness, and gently asked me to come in and separate the seed potatoes—which, incidentally, were never planted.

The pressure was building for us to get out of our homes. One day my father, sister and I got on the train in Sandy Cove and went to Dunville, where my father searched for a temporary residence until a permanent one could be established with all of the people of Argentia in one community. I continued my studies for Grade XI, and near the end of June my good friend and neighbour took me in a dory and landed me on Riley's Point in Fox Harbour, so I could write my C.H.E. exams the following week. Every one of my friends were attending a wedding reception "up the pond" that evening, but I made the best of a bad bargain, and have never forgotten my good friend who took the time out to be helpful.

The bulldozers began to excavate our garden out in back and were in the process of surrounding our house. My father refused to move until he received some remuneration. And so time passed quickly until one day I saw my brother and his family pack their belongings and leave their home. The realization finally dawned. I was really going to leave this beautiful place and lose the friendliness of all my good neighbours. I went out to the "little store" which was my fathers carpenter shop, and which also housed our horse's carriage on which we oftimes rode; and for the first time I cried.

By this time my sisters were beginning to pack up some household goods and clothing. I began to look around to see the things we could not pack. There was the grazin' ground, and the big meadow! the land wash on the beach under our hill with the splittin' tables, the store for the dry fish, and the smaller store for trawls and lines; there was the flake, Point Roche and the big rock out in the water on which we sat as the waves washed up around us in the summer; the motor boat, dory and flat. There dug into the hill was our cellar, which was warm in winter for the vegetables and cold in summer for the perishables.

I came up the hill—there was Mrs. Hunt's garden which our father had bought, our big garden behind the house in which we made hay in the summer, and in which we went slidin' in the winter, and across which we went to visit Mrs. Martha. There was our ground cellar made out of sods in which we kept the cabbage in winter; there was the front garden, the yard and the woodpile.

There was the barn, my favourite—how I loved that building—built, I supposed, by my grandfather. It had side steps going up in the front of a large hay loft, where in summer we had swings and sang "I Wish I Were Single Again;" and up there too was the old chest that came from Ireland. In the floor, there was a hole for throwing down hay in the winter to the cattle. Bernard, my cousin, fell down there when he was about 2 or 3 years old, but the fall must not have hurt him as he was very bright when he grew up. On the lower floor of that stable were stalls for the horse, the calf and the cow, and on the other side a door opened into the sheep house.

I went further down the road to the brook garden and the cabbage garden. How many times had I gone there with my father when he planted seed! I went to the Cove Hill where all the young people congregated, down over the Hill to the "Green" where we played ball, and on to the Cove where Rose and I stole her grandfather's flat and suffered the consequences. No, none of these things could be packed. One day I went to the cemetery where my mother had been buried eleven years before, and I talked to her as if she were still alive. I still remember most of what I said to her. I did not know then that even her remains would have to be moved to make way for the machinery of war.

The final day came in August 1941. They sent a truck to move our possessions. There was no time for grief. Everyone was occupied. We took the train to Dunville to where my father had found the temporary home, while he and my brothers went along with the truck. When we arrived my father was putting up the beds by the dim light of a lamp, as the house had no electricity. A week later my sisters and I returned to have a last look at our house. It was bulldozed to the ground!

That September I went to the Academy of Our Lady of Mercy in St. John's to continue my studies. By this time it was finally agreed that the Argentia community would settle in Freshwater.

So began the task of building a permanent home. There were no supplies or suppliers, so my father and some neighbours from Argentia decided to charter a vessel to bring them in from St Alban's, Bay D'Espoir. My sister was teaching school there and she negotiated with the local people. Those who lived through those times understand about the lack of communications—no phones—only letters and telegrams. So the pink messages were going to Bay D'Espoir.

In St. John's I was anxious and curious about what was taking place. My sister wrote and informed me that the vessel had left twelve days ago, and had not arrived. Finally on October 1, 1941 it arrived, but had not had enough space for all of the supplies. My father hoped the remainder would come on the *Burgeo*. On October 8, 1941, my father began operations. He built a "shack" down in the woods in Freshwater, and he and two men lived there during that long cold winter while they built their homes. Some mornings when they awoke, they were almost frozen with the cold.

When I returned for the Christmas holidays, my cousin walked me up the street to where the house was being constructed. When I turned in I went to my knees in mud and water; the road which was being built was not completed. It made me happy to see the progress being made. That Christmas the first Mass in the Church in Freshwater—Midnight Mass—was celebrated by Father Dee. My sisters and I walked down from Dunville to attend. In February 1942 the house was finished and our family moved from the residence in Dunville to the new home in Freshwater.

So a new life began for me—for all of us. Things could never be the same. New friendships had been formed, and as I went my way in St. John's, my eyes were always focused to see a face from Argentia.....Betty, how are you? Olive, where do you live? That boy in uniform is from Argentia ... a lingering longing for the old familiar faces.

Fifty years later a couple of friends and I went to visit an old friend somewhere in the United States. We saw a grey-haired lady who beckoned us to come in. When we entered she joined her hands and said "Thank you, Jesus." We all knew what she was thinking—by what strange paths each of has been led on our journey since we left Argentia. Truly, "The old order changes, giving place to the new, and God fulfils himself in many ways."

***Mrs. Rose Roche had a rather touching story to tell. A deep trench had been dug in front of their home with just a plank across to gain access to the road. They had one small child and were expecting another in a couple of months.***

In July of '41 they had to leave their new home to move to Smith's Point, into a house which had been vacant for years and which they had to share with another displaced family. It was in this house that her new baby was born, since our hospital in Argentia was now out of bounds. Asked if any of her possessions had been damaged during the move, she told me a rocking chair her husband had given her when her first baby was born had been broken almost beyond repair.

When her new baby was only three weeks old they received notice to leave Smith's Point, as construction of the Army Base in Marquise had now begun. In September she moved to South East Placentia to live with her parents for the winter; but because they had a large family, and her own children were getting older and needed more space, Mrs. Roche rented rooms with another family there who had a larger house.

In the meantime her husband, who was employed by the Railway at Argentia, had engaged carpenters to build their new house in Freshwater. Since he was living with his sister, he also worked on the house himself when time permitted. He had very little opportunity to visit his family in South East, so in the early summer of '42 they moved with the two babies into their partly built home, with one room serving as kitchen and bedroom for themselves and their children.

As she told me her story we both wondered whether, if this situation occurred today, the people would tolerate all the hardship and inconvenience endured by the people of Argentia at that time.

✣ ✣ ✣

*Mrs. Margaret McGrath's story was very similar to the previous one. A deep trench had also been dug around their house, leaving them on a small island, and they had to walk a narrow plank to leave their home.*

Mrs. McGrath and her husband, with their small daughter and elderly father, left their home in August and like the Roches, moved into a vacant house on Smith's Point, where they remained until October. Because alternate housing was altogether unavailable by then, her father and her husband built a two- bedroom shed on their plot in Freshwater, where on December 16 their second child was born; the hospital in Argentia now admitted Americans only.

The following spring her 69-year-old father, with the help of her husband (who was also employed on the Base) began building their new home, and they moved in the following September. A period of thirteen months had elapsed since leaving their comfortable home in Argentia.

✣ ✣ ✣

*Mrs. Rose Smith was in her late teens when their home was expropriated.*

When the evacuation date approached, her widowed mother, with the assistance of family members who were still at home, packed all of their household possessions, dismantled their beds, rolled up and secured their mattresses and bedding, and awaited the arrival of the moving truck. However, the truck did nor arrive for two or three days, so at night they had to unpack their mattresses and bedding and sleep on the floors of the kitchen and living rooms.

They then went to live to a vacant house in Dunville, about 3 or 4 miles distant; they stayed there until shortly before Christmas, when they were able to move into their new home in Freshwater.

Mrs. Smith (who was Rose Griffin at the time) had secured work with the Avalon Telephone Company in Marquise. Her attachment to her former home was so strong that when the weather permitted, she took her lunch to the now-deserted house a mile distant, as construction activity had not yet begun there. One day as she approached the house she saw that a rosebush which had been growing near the door had been uprooted and pushed over an embankment. She experienced at that moment a great feeling of sadness, and with it the realization that construction work had begun and she would no longer be able to visit what to her had been "Home Sweet Home."

She continued to work in Marquise and commute to Dunville as best she could, sometimes walking and sometimes getting a "lift" from a friend or a relative. This continued until the temporary living quarters were built for the employees of what came to be known as Fort McAndrew.

✣ ✣ ✣

***Mrs. Margaret (Griffin) Smith died in May 1991 at the age of 74. The following is her story, as told to her children over many years.***

We had just recently built and moved into our new house on Smith's Point when we found out we'd have to leave Argentia. My husband Cornelius (Con) was working in the Buchans mines, but he came home even before the Base started. He wanted to come back to set potatoes and turnips in the spring. Most of the men had to go away to work in those days, so they were delighted when they found out they'd get jobs on the Base. Con was among the first crowd to be hired on. That was the good side of it, everyone got steady work. I don't think anyone realized at first how much of a difference the Base would make in our lives.

We hated having to give up our homes. Everyone was in the same boat—where were we going to find another place to live? We had to leave Argentia in the height of winter. We rented a vacant house in Dunville. Three families moved in together—myself and Con and the baby, Peggy, who had only been born in October; my mother, Maggie Griffin, and the three children she had at home—Agatha, Rose and Matt; and Uncle Mick Griffin and his seven children.

The house was big and drafty. There was a wide seam underneath the bedroom window, and although we tried to keep it covered, on bad nights snow would come in on the bed. We used to worry about the baby, she was very small and delicate. I remember, some mornings we'd get up and there'd be a layer of snow on the floor.

When myself and Con and the baby moved down to Freshwater it was still winter. My mother had a house by then and we went in with her at first. The men drew lots for land, and we ended up with a spot up past the top of Settlement Hill, on the First Beach Road. Con had a shed pulled up from Argentia and then we moved into that, and that's where we lived while he was building the house. It was no better than the place in Dunville. When it started to warm up a bit there would sometimes be fog inside the house.

We bought a piece of land down in the middle of Settlement Hill from Cyril Kelly, and as soon as a couple of rooms were finished, we moved in. It was spring by then. We had five moves within a year, four within a few months, and with a small baby, it wasn't easy.

We got used to it over time, but things were never the same. We missed Argentia and the way of life we had down there. At least all the men had jobs now and we were better off; still, I don't know if that was enough to make up for having to leave our homes.

---

*Note: Margaret and Rose Griffin were sisters who married cousins, Cornelius and Gerald Smith. Although she tended to downplay the trauma of the move, all throughout her life my mother (Margaret) never considered any place else but Argentia her home, and she loved to go driving around the Base, pointing out to us children the places she had known and telling us stories about her childhood.—(Peggy Krachun)*

❖ ❖ ❖

*Mrs. Madonna Cleary was fourteen years old when her parents received their notice to evacuate their home in June 1941.*

Her father decided to move his family of seven to South East Placentia, where he had secured a vacant house. He placed all of their possessions in a motor boat and then had to take the long route around Pt. Latine, in through Placentia Gut and up the South East Arm to their destination. She told me that her mother had brought all of her house flowers, and she still remembers seeing them placed on the kitchen couch as the boat took them and their possessions away from their home and familiar surroundings to live amongst strangers.

For some time she missed her friends and neighbours, but after starting school in September she made new friends, got to know her new neighbours, and soon adjusted to her new surroundings.

❖ ❖ ❖

*Mrs. Michael O'Reilly (Clara) kept a sort of diary, and her account is typical of the experience of so many who had been dispossessed, especially those who had to make two moves:*

## 1941

May 8—Went over to Smith's Pt. in truck to see house. Men taking over wood.

May 13—Almost all furniture, beds and stove, etc. brought over, except one bed and parlour stove. Went over in truck and returned. Josephine and self remained all night. Jim and Paul came later and slept on floor.

May 14—Rain. Stayed all day picking up what remained. Bulldozers and tractors working in garden behind barn. Josephine and self stayed again at night.

May 15—Rain and more rain. Food short, nothing only vegetable soup and raisin bread. Josephine decided to go at 11 o'clock a.m. Remained alone in house still packing. Truck arrived for goods at 4 p.m. Raining and blowing. All gone except piano and table. Wrote Joan while waiting for car. Mr. Ned Sampson's house demolished while I wrote. Also Mike Houlihan's pulled over, but not demolished. Bulldozers in meadow behind house. Raining a deluge. Car stopped below Bruce's. Had to walk with slippers and high heel gaiters. Paul brought suit case. Brian took fur coat and parcel. Carried teapot and Mary's coat. Umbrella useless. Car window broken, rain drifting in. Car stopped distance from house. Had to walk in and carry luggage. Still raining. Had to put up beds and clear up. Retired 1:00 a.m. after the hardest day in my life up to that time.

May 27—House burned.

Oct. 30—Left Marquise. All goods gone at 3 p.m. Waiting for car which did not come. Walked to Mrs. Mary Hunt's. Took car there, drove to North East bridge which was broken, got out and walked the remaining way.

Oct. 31—In bed all day until evening.

Nov. 4—Foundation of house in Freshwater laid.

Dec. 4—Family came to live in house.

Dec. 16—I left Dunville.

Dec. 18—Tom went to San.

Dec. 24—First Mass in New Argentia, Midnight, 1941.

✤ ✤ ✤

*The most poignant story of all was that of an elderly couple who had recently moved into a new bungalow, where they had expected to live out their remaining years.*

**Mr. and Mrs. Albert O'Reilly:**

Then came the reality that they would have to pack up, leave Newfoundland and join their family in the U.S. In the meantime, while moving in with a family further from the construction site, the old lady's possessions were being conveyed in boxes by horse and slide to their new location. The horse took fright for some reason, upsetting the slide, and the contents of the boxes—which included her pieces of lustreware and other most prized possessions—were smashed into little pieces.

Soon afterwards the family they moved in with had to vacate their home and go to Dunville, so the old couple moved in with a family in Marquise until their affairs with the Compensation Board were settled. Later they set out by train for Boston, but the old gentleman became ill and was taken off the train at Grand Falls, where he passed away. No doubt this unexpected upheaval in his life, at his advanced age, shortened his days.

❖ ❖ ❖

*The former residents of Argentia deserve some recognition for the suffering they endured during that difficult event in their lives.*

Our present Mayor, Mr. Joseph Joy, is now endeavouring to set up archives in the Town Hall, and it is hoped that he will receive the necessary co-operation and assistance from both levels of Government, as well as from the American Government and the people of the area. This memorial will be a source of knowledge for visitors and tourists interested in the events that transpired during that critical period in history. But more importantly, it will be a source of pride to the descendants of the people of Argentia.

# Epilogue

WHILE WE WERE STILL LIVING IN ARGENTIA A COMMUNIQUE FROM Lieutenant Stephens, U.S. Navy Commander, dated July 27, 1941, informed Father Dee that in the near future it would be necessary to enforce a number of regulations which would hamper freedom of movement. Since we were at war the necessity of military security was quite understandable; however, it did nothing to ease the trauma being experienced by those people who had been uprooted from their homes but were still living nearby.

Privately-owned boats would not be permitted to land or come within a thousand yards of the Naval Station. All persons living or working on the Base would be required to have passes showing their photograph, fingerprints and signature. Visitors, with the exception of high-ranking military or government personnel, would not be admitted. People having official business would be allowed on the Base only when escorted by a sentry. This last regulation prevented our attending Church, and so we finally realized Argentia was no longer our home.

After the war the rules were relaxed somewhat and visitors were permitted, but only if they were sponsored and accompanied by someone, either military or civilian, who held a pass.

Just recently two members of my family came home on vacation and of course wished to visit Marquise, where we had been born and raised. We were pleasantly surprised to be given the necessary pass to enter the Base, but were told that since we had no sponsor, a military escort would go with us. Having a Marine with a walkie-talkie ride with us in our car amused us, but we found him most patient, courteous and helpful, since we did not have to worry whether we were on territory that was out of bounds.

Although it was impossible to pinpoint the exact location of our house, for a while we relived the past. We wondered where the marsh had been where we had picked bakeapples, blueberries, partridge berries and marshberries in their different seasons. Where were the hayfields, where after the first day's drying in the sun we gathered the hay into mounds we called "haycocks", to be spread again next morning, weather permitting? Where was the large garden in which Mother grew such a variety of vegetables—enough to last until the next harvest season? And the raspberry bushes, the berries that, with a generous serving of fresh cream, had made such a delicious dessert?

In front of us lay the wide expanse of Placentia Bay which neither man nor machine could alter, and which we had viewed all our lives in all its different moods. We were not lucky enough that day to see one more glorious sunset. No doubt we would not have taken it so much for granted as we had back then; now we can see it only through the eyes of our memory. We wondered where our school had been, where teachers had laid a solid foundation for the careers we eventually followed; nor could we locate the site of the Church that had played such a significant role in our Christian upbringing.

We visited the Shag Pond—so near our home. Still there were the familiar rocks our small brothers had perched on as they fished for prickle-backs. This pond had in winter provided an excellent outdoor rink, and in summer given us the opportunity to try our hand at rowing a dory borrowed from an obliging neighbour.

We then drove to Salmonier, that part of Marquise where our maternal grandparents had lived. In the distance we could see Red Island, Fox Island, The Isaacs, Ship Harbour Point (off which history had been made), the Sound, Silver Cliff, and Hall's Point where our ancestor John Hall had settled on his arrival from England—places of interest to us still, and very much like meeting old friends again.

We wondered if the Northern Lights, or Aurora Borealis, could be seen as plainly now as when we had watched them in spring and autumn—beautiful displays of green lights, flickering and dancing in the night sky. Even the moon was not forgotten in our reminiscing; it had literally been our guiding light then, because there were no street lights. We remembered how our mother had waited for a full moon so she could visit a friend who lived at some distance. (Very few people could afford flashlights at that time. Our grandfathers had used kerosene lanterns and their forefathers had used a fire brand, or bran—a piece of wood lighted in the stove on leaving the house).*

No doubt change is inevitable, but a significant and unexpected change had to be made by the residents of Argentia in 1941. By being uprooted from our native soil, transplanted to a new environment and, I may add, a new culture, we had to begin a different way of life. However, we do not harbour any bitterness; on the contrary, we have a feeling of pride in the knowledge that Argentia played such an important role in the winning of the Battle of the Atlantic and consequently the defeat of Germany, and because of this has earned a place in Newfoundland and world history.

This story has been written in order to help keep alive for our descendants the sacrifice we were called upon to make for the cause of justice and peace, and for this may we always be remembered.

* It is from this custom that we get the term "brand new" or "bran-new," which means quite new, as if fresh from the fire. Should the bran burn out before a person reached his destination, he dropped in to some house en route for a fresh bran. This led to the saying which I still remember, "You must have come only for a bran" should a friend make a rather short visit. Sometimes when we use the term "brand new" to describe an article, we may visualize an ancestor wending his way home in the darkness, "brandishing" his torch. It is rather unlikely now that a friend would remark after you paid a short visit to his home, "you must have come for a bran." And so lifestyles change and old customs give way to new.

# Appendix I

Altogether 108 families were evacuated from Argentia in 1941. That figure does not include some people listed in Appendix II who had left Argentia previously but still owned property there.

**HOUSEHOLDERS OF ARGENTIA WHOSE PROPERTY WAS EXPROPRIATED**

Ann Bruce
Anthony Bruce
Ellen Bruce
Joseph Byrd
Sarah Byrd
Thomas Byrd
Francis Cleary
John Cleary
Richard and Ellen Cleary
Michael Cooney
Thomas Cooney
John Corcoran
Edward Cunningham
John Cunningham
Lucy Cunningham
Margaret Davis
Bernard Dollmont Sr.
Bernard Dollmont Jr.
John Dollmont
William Dollmont
Alexander Dunphy
Martha Dunphy
Michael Dunphy
Patrick Dunphy
Michael Fitzpatrick
Patrick Follett
Caroline Foran
Pauline Foran
Edward Griffin
Margaret Griffin
Michael Griffin
Robert Griffin
Ellen Healey
Richard Healey
James Hickey
Ronald Hickey
Edward Houlihan
Michael Houlihan
Andrew Hunt
Ellen Hunt
Mary Hunt
Michael Hunt Sr.
Thomas Hunt
Philip Joy
Lucy Keats
John Kelly
Michael Kelly
Paul Kelly
Thomas Kelly (of John)
Thomas F. Kelly
Joseph Kerrivan
Patrick Ledwell
James Leonard
William Lynch
Alex Maher
Daniel Maher
Frank Maher
Kevin Maher
Marcellus Maher
Michael Maher
William Maher
Ann McCue
James McGrath
John McGrath (of Richard)
Hannah Meade
Robert and Lucy Meade
Christopher Mulrooney
Patrick Murphy
Joachim Murray
Margaret Murray
Patrick Murray Jr.
Albert and Theresa O'Reilly
Dennis O'Reilly
Michael and Clara O'Reilly
Patrick O'Reilly Sr.
Philip O'Reilly
Philip O'Reilly (Marquise)
Philip B. O'Reilly
Philip W. O'Reilly
Dominic O'Reilly
Alphonsus Power
Bernard Power

John Power
Leo Power
Michael Power
Richard Power (of Richard)
Thomas Power (of Richard)
Thomas Power (of Michael)
Hugh Roche
James and Mary Roche
James and Rose Roche
Peter Roche
Thomas Roche
Edward Sampson
John Sampson
Joseph Sampson
Martin Sampson
Mary Agnes Sampson
Anthony Silver
Alex Smith
Anthony Smith
Bridget Ann Smith
Constance Smith
Cornelius Smith
Henry and Mary Ann Smith
Henry Smith Sr.
William Smith Jr.
Julia Walsh

## Appendix II

The average amount awarded to Marquise householders was $6,000 each, and to Argentia Peninsula householders, $3,000 each. Most of the larger amounts listed below were compensation paid for businesses, fishing premises and rental property.

**COMPENSATION AWARDED TO MARQUISE RESIDENTS**

| NAME | AWARD |
|---|---|
| Dominic O'Reilly | $1,900.00 |
| Daniel Maher | 4,960.00 |
| Thomas Cooney | 6,760.00 |
| Michael Cooney | 9,015.00 |
| Fergus Ryan | 2,600.00 |
| Thomas Hunt | 3,365.00 |
| Bernard Dollmont, Sr. | 5,065.00 |
| James C. Smith | 2,225.00 |
| Johannah Smith | 21,945.00 |
| Edward Griffin | 565.00 |
| Estate of John Furlong | 6,520.00 |
| Estate of William Fitzpatrick | 3,200.00 |
| John Maher (of John) | 6,315.00 |
| Michael Fitzpatrick | 8,970.00 |
| Martha Dunphy | 6,545.00 |
| Alexander Dunphy | 6,995.00 |
| Francis Fitzpatrick | 2,760.00 |
| Michael J. Smith | 10,430.00 |
| Ellen Hunt | 6,520.00 |
| Patrick J. Dunphy | 10,850.00 |
| Michael Dunphy | 10,145.00 |
| Estate of Mary Ann Lawlor | 5,360.00 |
| Milton Smith | 5,410.00 |
| Alexander Smith, Sr. | 4,980.00 |
| Estate of Peter Smith | 1,395.00 |
| Lucy Houlihan | 2,765.00 |
| Josephine Penney | 3,565.00 |
| Joseph Byrd | 2,460.00 |
| Estate of Patrick Dunphy | 4,785.00 |
| William Maher | 5,440.00 |
| Joachim Murray | 4,805.00 |
| Estate of Maurice Murray | 5,500.00 |
| Daniel Murray | 5,740.00 |
| Margaret Murray (Wife of Patrick) | 3,165.00 |
| Patrick Murray, Jr. | 2,920.00 |
| Bernard Dollmont, Jr. | 2,135.00 |
| Joseph Sampson | 7,600.00 |
| John Cooney | 2,015.00 |
| Michael Joseph & Kevin Maher | 6,815.00 |

| | |
|---|---|
| John Hanrahan | 1,060.00 |
| Patrick Follett | 2,750.00 |
| Estate of Michael A. Smith | 5,720.00 |
| Mary Hunt | 6,215.00 |
| Margaret Griffin | 7,300.00 |
| John Dollmont | 2,095.00 |
| James Hickey | 3,915.00 |
| Mary Follett | 425.00 |
| Patrick & John O'Reilly (of Edward) | 4,620.00 |
| Thomas Cooney (Award #2) | 950.00 |
| Estate of John J. Maher | 6,815.00 |
| Francis Maher | 675.00 |
| Joseph Kerrivan | 1,120.00 |
| William M. Smith, Sr. | 4,385.00 |
| Thomas Kelly (of John) | 13,985.00 |
| Estate of Alexander Maher | 6,955.00 |
| Estate of John Dunphy | 725.00 |
| Raymond Dunphy | 850.00 |
| Estate of James Maher (of John) | 6,135.00 |
| Marcellus Maher | 8,420.00 |
| John Kelly | 9,970.00 |
| Paul Kelly | 11,375.00 |
| William P. Smith | 2,180.00 |
| William M. Smith, Jr. | 1,645.00 |
| Henry J. Smith | 5,070.00 |
| Estate of William Foley | 6,525.00 |
| Estate of Patrick Houlihan | 2,165.00 |
| Julia Walsh | 2,810.00 |
| James Smith (of Peter) | 3,210.00 |
| William M. Smith (of Michael) | 1,365.00 |
| Estate of Cornelius Smith | 6,845.00 |
| Cornelius Smith (of Cornelius) | 1,510.00 |
| Henry Smith (of Cornelius) | 1,360.00 |
| Philip O'Reilly | 12,580.00 |
| John Foley (of James) | 3,040.00 |
| Alexander Smith (of Peter) | 9,340.00 |
| Mary Houlihan Murphy | 575.00 |
| Michael Griffin | 3,795.00 |
| Bride Kelly | 425.00 |
| Thomas M. Smith (of Peter) | 5,515.00 |
| Estate of Edward Walsh | 5,055.00 |
| Estate of Ann Hall Hunt | 2,070.00 |
| Michael Hunt | 5,125.00 |
| William Dollmont | 1,720.00 |
| Roman Catholic Episcopal Corporation (Marquise School) | 6,740.00 |
| Peter Smith (of Peter) | 250.00 |
| TOTAL | $417,461.00 |

## COMPENSATION AWARDED TO ARGENTIA PENINSULA RESIDENTS

| NAME | AWARD |
|---|---|
| John Cunningham | $1,920.00 |
| Philip B. & Mary O'Reilly | 3,400.00 |
| Ellen Bruce | 4,000.00 |
| Mary & James Roche | 3,000.00 |
| Estate of Patrick Sampson | 2,650.00 |
| Edward Sampson | 2,750.00 |
| Lucy Sparrow Cuningham | 2,650.00 |
| Hugh Roche | 1,640.00 |
| Alphonsus Power | 3,080.00 |
| John Sullivan | 8,277.00 |
| Patrick Murphy | 2,230.00 |
| Pauline Power Foran | 4,040.00 |
| Andrew Hunt, Senior | 1,860.00 |
| Andrew Hunt, Junior | 1,880.00 |
| Albert B. & Theresa Evans O'Reilly | 5,250.00 |
| John Sampson | 2,385.00 |
| Mary Ellen Dwyer | 420.00 |
| Thomas Byrd | 450.00 |
| Patrick Vaters | 4,245.00 |
| Robert Griffin | 1,815.00 |
| William Houlihan | 1,500.00 |
| Estate of William Sampson | 1,755.00 |
| James Leonard | 820.00 |
| Bridget Cunningham | 720.00 |
| Estate of Lawrence Cleary | 970.00 |
| Francis Cleary | 3,570.00 |
| Estate of Martin M. Sampson (per Mary Sampson) | 2,860.00 |
| Michael J. Smith | 240.00 |
| Lucy M. Keats | 2,700.00 |
| Anthony Bruce | 225.00 |
| Mary Bridget Bruce | 130.00 |
| Frank Evans | 2,685.00 |
| Francis Maher | 13,080.00 |
| Ann Bruce | 3,200.00 |
| Estate of Thomas Cleary | 1,975.00 |
| Dennis Cleary | 90.00 |
| Thomas F.Kelly | 5,500.00 |
| William Cleary | 195.00 |
| John Cleary | 1,250.00 |
| John Cochrane | 280.00 |
| Estate of James Houlihan | 5,350.00 |
| Richard Healey | 13,500.00 |
| Caroline Foran | 2,285.00 |
| Michael Houlihan | 2,840.00 |

| | |
|---|---|
| William Lynch | 3,565.00 |
| Michael T. Kelly | 3,180.00 |
| Christopher Mulrooney & Philip Joy | 2,030.00 |
| Sarah Byrd | 2,530.00 |
| Patrick Ledwell | 3,535,00 |
| Estate of John Meade (Mrs. Hannah Meade) | 4,010.00 |
| John McGrath (of James) | 370.00 |
| James J. McGrath | 3,525.00 |
| Philip J. O'Reilly | 3,435.00 |
| Robert and Lucy Meade | 1,965.00 |
| Ellen Healey (Administratrix of Estate of Michael Healey) | 14,150.00 |
| Estate of Michael McGrath (Per John McGrath of Richard) | 1,780.00 |
| Dennis O'Reilly | 7,730.00 |
| Estate of John O'Reilly | 2,370.00 |
| Estate of Patrick O'Reilly | 2,090.00 |
| Ann McCue | 3,090.00 |
| Thomas O'Reilly (of Philip, Point Moll) | 2,680.00 |
| Estate of Austin Roche | 2,270.00 |
| Estate of Patrick Cleary (Per Richard Cleary) | 455.00 |
| Ellen Cleary (wife of Richard) | 1,510.00 |
| Martin W. Sampson | 3,940.00 |
| Joseph Byrd | 640.00 |
| Estate of Patrick Lynch | 1.030.00 |
| Estate of Patrick Evans | 870.00 |
| Thomas Murray | 2,400.00 |
| Thomas Bruce, Jr. | 850.00 |
| Michael Power | 2,415.00 |
| John Power, Sr. | 4,300.00 |
| " " " Award #2 | 452.00 |
| Leo Power | 3,215.00 |
| Laura O'Reilly Harnett | 150.00 |
| Rose Power | 1,370.00 |
| Bernard Power | 2,590.00 |
| Peter Roche, Sr. | 3,000.00 |
| Thomas Roche | 2,500.00 |
| Edward Cleary | 2,200.00 |
| Patrick Sampson | 610.00 |
| Estate of John Sparrow | 1,850.00 |
| Anthony Silver | 1,615.00 |
| William Duke | 525.00 |
| Mary Ryan | 2,240.00 |
| Thomas Ryan | 100.00 |
| James Baird, Limited | 8,210.00 |
| James Laing | 300.00 |

| | |
|---|---|
| Thomas Power (of Richard) | 4,440.00 |
| William Power (of Richard) | 1,380.00 |
| Philip W. O'Reilly | 2,840.00 |
| Estate of John Roche | 1,900.00 |
| Estate of Robert Sparrow | 2,475.00 |
| Richard Power (of Richard) | 2,775.00 |
| Thomas Power (of Michael) | 2,700.00 |
| Paul Kelly | 10,890.00 |
| Mary Miller | 1,310.00 |
| Louise Doody | 9,200.00 |
| Michael & Clara O'Reilly | 3,225.00 |
| Estate of George Sparrow | 600.00 |
| Estate of Thomas J. Power (Per Alice Power, Administratrix) | 2,645.00 |
| Estate of Thomas Walsh | 480.00 |
| Barnaby Fennessey | 420.00 |
| Estate of Andrew Sparrow | 2,570.00 |
| Patrick O'Reilly (of Patrick) | 160.00 |
| James O'Reilly | 290.00 |
| John Roche | 1,490.00 |
| Roman Catholic Episcopal Corporation | 87,888.80 |
| Estate of John Meade | 845.00 |
| North American Fisheries, Limited | 35,618.00 |
| Thomas S. Keats | 2,850.00 |
| William J. Walsh | 1,000.00 |
| Kevin Cleary | 1,718.00 |
| Peter Meade | 1,214.00 |
| Estate of Alphonsus Keats & Thomas S. Keats | 2,500.00 |
| Estate of George King | 530.00 |
| Philip O'Reilly | 4,015.00 |
| Andrew Roche | 75.00 |
| Thomas J. Power | 330.00 |
| Estate of Thomas McCue | 320.00 |
| Estate of Francis Walsh | 420.00 |
| George Hollett | 75.00 |
| James J. McGrath (Award #2) | 440.00 |
| Michael Power (Award #2) | 374.28 |
| Philip O'Reilly (Award #2) | 665.00 |
| Margaret Davis | 34,817.20 |
| TOTAL | $465,439.53 |

# Appendix III

In recent years there has been an upsurge of interest in the Argentia episode of our history. Below is a newspaper account of a meeting which took place in 1986:

Page 12, The Evening Telegram, Saturday, May 10, 1986

## *Conference address a reminder*

## Argentia people have not forgotten how they were forced from their land

By ANNE WHALEN
Telegram Correspondent

FRESHWATER — Although it has been almost 40 years since the Commission of Government forced the people of Argentia and Marquis off their land on the Argentia Peninsula, the people of that area have not forgotten. They have not forgotten how Sir Winston Churchill offered it to President Franklin D. Roosevelt as part of a deal which saw England get 50 used warships; or how they had to move out of their homes, most of them with no place to go.

They will not forget the heroic efforts of parish priest Father Dee, or their lawyer, Phil Lewis. Long gone, but not forgotten, is the paltry sum of money they got for their land, houses and other property — not enough to build a new house let alone furnish it with the amenities of their former dwellings.

Now, 40 years later, they pose the questions: Are we not in the same situation as the Japanese Canadians who were forced out of their homes and land? When the 99-year lease expires, will the land be returned to the former owners to pass on as a legacy to the next generation?

These questions were part of an address delivered by a native of Argentia, Eileen Houlihan, to a group of people attending a conference studying the Commission of Government as it existed in Newfoundland in the years preceding Confederation. Sponsored by the Newfoundland Archives, it included a group of Memorial University students and professors; a visiting professor from the University of Western Ontario, as well as representatives of the Newfoundland Archives and other parties. The conference was in Argentia and Freshwater on a field study of the effects of some of the decisions made by the Commission of Government. That included a tour of the Argentia area, a visit to the Freshwater cemetery, and finally discussion of the whole issue at a meeting in the Freshwater Community Centre.

The first speaker for the afternoon was May Maher, who read a series of letters between the parish priest and the government concerning the movement of bodies out of the Argentia graveyard. Mrs. Maher explained how the United States Navy wanted the graves removed, and how the people turned to their government, which refused, saying that the people should request assistance from the U.S. Navy. The Navy built the new cemetery, moved all the bodies in the night into a mass grave, and then built a road to the cemetery.

"The epic of Argentia would fill volumes," began the next speech by former resident Anne McGrath. She spoke on life in Argentia from 1934-1940.

In talking about the announcement that the Americans would build a base there, she said: "Our people welcomed the news. It would be something different, a new source of employment. But then came the dawning of reality and the long lonely funerals in the night as our people realized what was happening. With them went the values, skills, and knowledge of generations...

"The Americans were warm, friendly and generous and they were loved. It was the government who left us with no place to go and no provision for reimbursement because of the Emergency Powers Defense Act... But we rose above the difficulty and marched into the future... we do not have a strong and enduring bitterness — we stand on truth."

Eileen Houlihan, the third speaker, told about how the people actually were forced out of their homes; how they moved to Freshwater and tried to get on with life. After questioning the rightful ownership of the land when the American lease is terminated, she said: "We made a sacrifice in the cause of world peace."

Everyone agreed that indeed they did, and speakers were asked questions concerning legal, educational, political and even moral matters — and their answers proved to be just what the conference was looking for.

Dr. Jim Overton of MUN, chairman of the conference, said "...the field study was invaluable to the conference and each person will be interested in different facts of the Argentia issue. It will definitely encourage further research."

The people of Argentia at the meeting were glad to get the opportunity to let some people know what really happened to them during the confusion of the Second World War. For them, it was more than a government forcing them out of house and home — it was the destruction of a way of life they loved.